Maintenance and Reliability Lubrication 101
Keeping It Simple

By Ricky Smith & David A. Martin

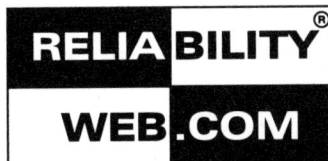

RELIABILITY WEB.COM®

Maintenance and Reliability Lubrication 101
Keeping It Simple

By Ricky Smith & David A. Martin

ISBN 978-0-9825163-2-4

Cover design by Patricia Serio
Cover photograph courtesy of Lubrication Engineers Inc. (www.le-inc.com)

For information: Reliabilityweb.com
www.reliabilityweb.com
PO Box 60075 Fort Myers, FL 33906
Toll Free: 888-575-1245, Office: 239-333-2500
E-mail: customerservice@reliabilityweb.com

10 9 8 7 6 5 4 3 2 1

TABLE OF CONTENTS

Lubrication accounts for a significant proportion of equipment failures. Improper lubrication practices are at the heart of many equipment reliability issues. Studies have shown that 70-85% of equipment failures are self induced, meaning that maintenance practices and processes are directly responsible for the failures. In a recent survey conducted online, companies responded that poor lubrication practices represent about 40% of maintenance-related self induced failures. In the same study, more than 80% of respondents stated that they consider lubrication to be a significant problem in their operation.

Lubrication is a required component in the operation of the majority of equipment:

- Gear reducers (Gears in general)
- Electric motors
- Chain drives
- Air compressors
- Pumps
- Anything with bearings
- Etc.

As such, it's obvious that proper lubrication is vital to the success of reliability and, in turn, operational assurance and cost control.

One of the main reasons that companies struggle with lubrication effectiveness is that they rely solely on standard Original Equipment Manufacturer's (OEM's) lubrication recommendations. Manufactures' recommendations do have their place, but there is much more to an effective lubrication program than what the manufacturer supplies. Additionally, lubrication programs are thought to be complicated and unobtainable. Granted, a lubrication program may take slightly more effort than your current program but it doesn't have to be complex, and improvements are achievable.

Developing an understanding of basic lubrication principles

and practices may be the largest part of moving towards improvements. First and foremost: **Discipline is the key to the success of any proactive maintenance program.**

This book will identify effective ways to bridge the gap between established and proven Best Practices and your current program. Combining the right lubrication activities with proper practices, a significant opportunity exists to use the lubrication function within maintenance to impact plant reliability.

The following survey on lubrication, and its impact on reliability, was completed in August 2005 in conjunction with Plant Services Magazine. Over 200 maintenance professionals participated in this survey. Although some companies are doing things right when it comes to lubrication, most are not. Follow along as the findings from each of the survey's questions is summarized.

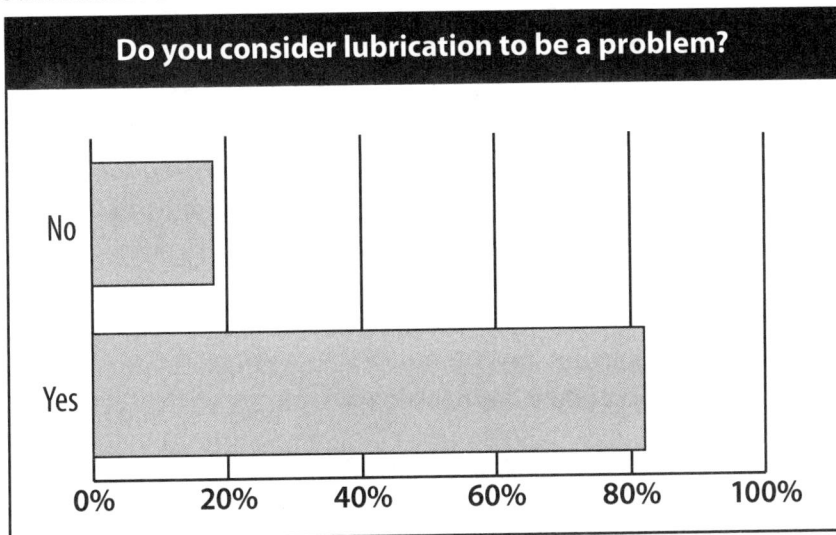

Do you consider lubrication to be a problem?

No	
Yes	

0%   20%   40%   60%   80%   100%

With over 80% of respondents stating lubrication is a problem in their operation, responses to this first question clearly show the significance of the lubrication problem. While the question does not attempt to identify what the problem is, we can assume that respondents have some ideas. Resolution, rather than identification, is the problem.

In what area do you have the most lubrication problems?

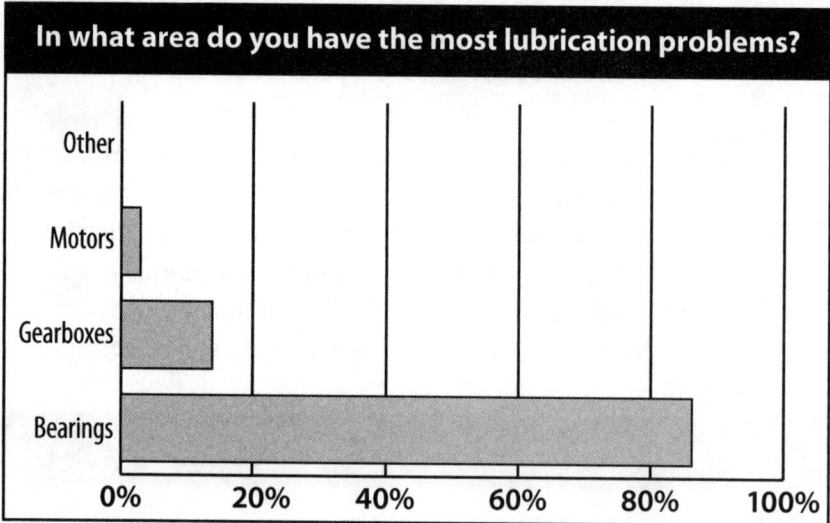

This question produced some interesting results. We would have thought that motors and gear reducers would have been a larger problem. As you can tell from the survey results, bearings are the largest problem in most organizations, with gear reducers a distant second. It also shows that in most organizations, motors (assuming that bearings do not include motor bearings) seem to have the least problem with lubrication.

With lubrication the leading cause of motor failure, it could be that the motor repair shops are not interpreting the whole story. Observation of a large motor repair facility indicates there are numerous motors that have failed as a result of lubrication, either by-passing a seal bearing in the motor, or from grease being pushed through the bearing and into the motor windings.

In most operations, the severity of the lubrication issue is overlooked. "In a reactive environment we do not focus on the real problems but on the problems that face us on a specific day".

Water Ingression

Motor Winding End-turns completely covered in grease due to Over-greasing

Unless root cause analysis is performed, it may not be fair to contribute bearing failure to lubrication. In order to understand the true problem with bearing failure, one must review the problem from storage, installation, and maintenance perspectives, as well as lubrication practices. Failures must be followed by a root cause investigation to ensure true causes of failure are addressed.

What percentage of your equipment downtime is related to lubrication?

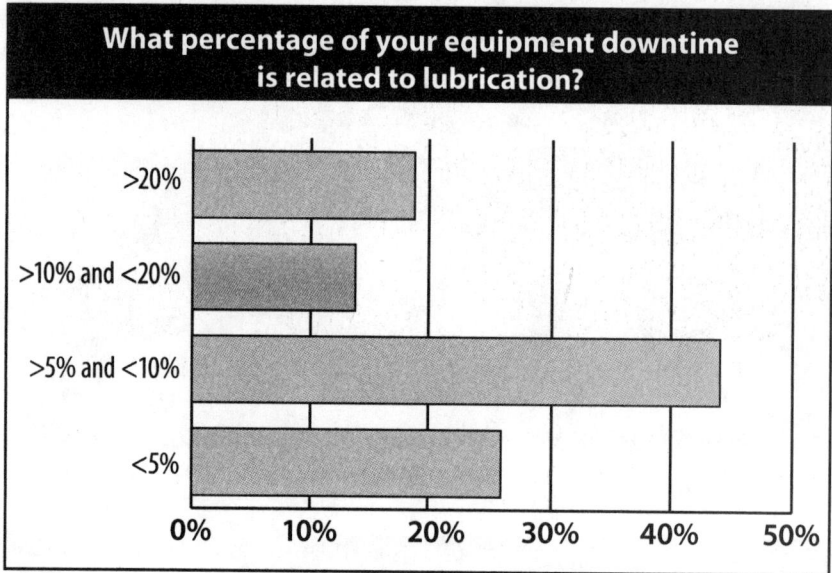

It is important for a company to know the percentage of their downtime related to lubrication. A separate study, completed prior to this questionnaire survey, found that most equipment downtime was related to production problems, not maintenance or reliability issues. With over 18% of companies having more than 20% of their equipment failures directly related to lubrication problems, think of the money lost every day. Companies state they don't have money for improvements, but with numbers like these, the money is there for improvement, someone just has to take the time to measure and communicate the losses.

It is apparent that 75% of those surveyed are aware of significant problems, an opportunity which can become an area for major cost savings. In getting support for improvements, it is important that you measure the cost of failures and the potential savings incurred by avoiding or deferring those failures. Be as accurate as you can with your presentation.

Equipment Failure Due to Lubrication. Courtesy of Alcoa, Mt Holly

How do you address the losses (cost and labor hours) incurred by lubrication? You begin with accurate data in order to quantify the size of the problem. You must determine root causes of failure in some detail (poor lubrication, contamination, the wrong type, too much, etc.), current maintenance practices, and a history of occurrences with this or similar equipment.

Then you calculate losses—capacity production losses based on downtime, labor losses/cost, and equipment repair/replacement cost. You could attribute inventory and administration costs but typically this gets a bit complex and is not required. In fact, you will likely find that "capacity lost" alone will more than cover any improvement cost. However, it is very important to show the loss of labor hours that can be better utilized performing proactive tasks, as well as the unnecessary cost for repair and/or replacement of equipment.

Do you have a person dedicated to lubrication?

No							
Yes							

0%   10%   20%   30%   40%   50%   60%

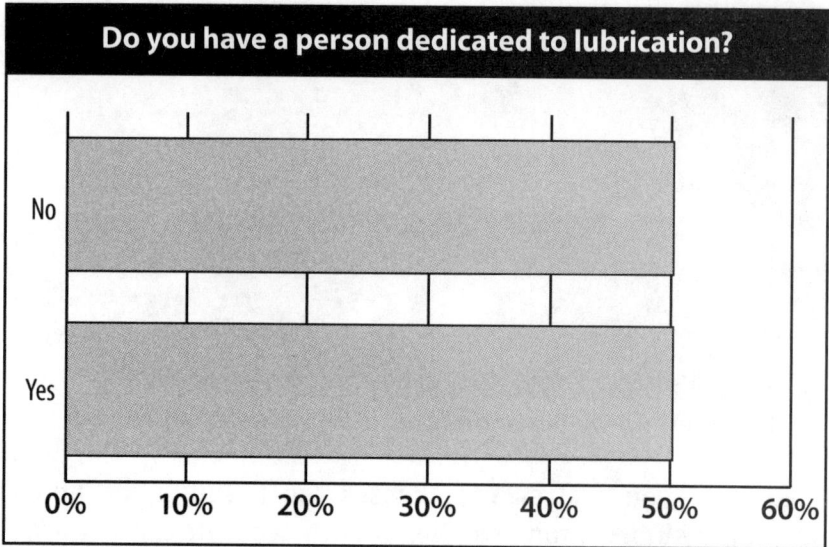

There are lubricators who do a great job and there are those that do a very poor job. However, no one comes to work with the expectation of failing. Poor practices are nearly 100% attributable to a lack of formal training or lack of clearly defined process expectations.

The survey indicates that having a person dedicated to lubrication does not ensure lubrication is performed correctly. In order for this person to perform their job to standard, they must be trained to the prerequisites of the job and then held accountable to that standard.

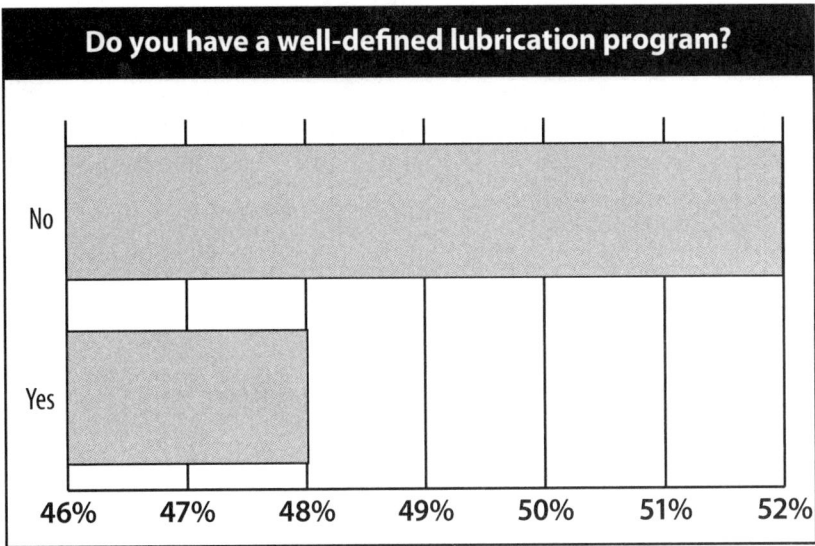

Do you have a well-defined lubrication program?

It is interesting to note that 52% of respondents stated no while 48% stated yes. Having a well defined lubrication program is key and the necessary first step to ensuring a successful lubrication program.

For this question, the difference between 48% and 52% is insignificant. What is significant is that over 30% of all respondents stated that at least 10% of their equipment downtime is related to lubrication issues. There is a high probability that the 30% of respondents with over 10% downtime are those who do not have a well defined lubrication program. Investing in one would prove invaluable.

At what skill level is your maintenance staff?

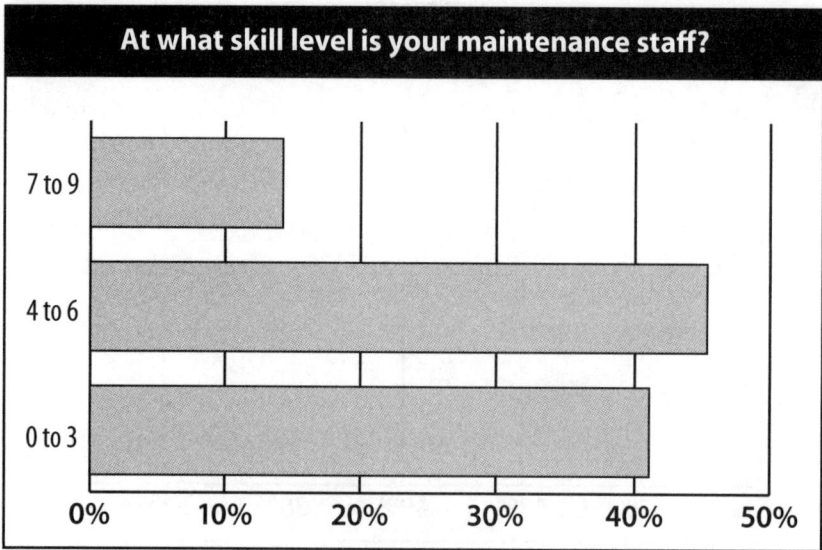

Over 40% of the respondents stated that the skill level of their maintenance staff is below a 3 (on a scale of 1-10 with 10 being the highest) in Lubrication.

If over 30% of companies have more than 10% of their downtime due to lubrication issues, then their low skill level in lubrication directly correlates to their downtime problem. If those organizations without dedicated lubricators utilize maintenance staff for lubrication needs, it becomes apparent that part of the solution to the downtime issue is to train people. Remember that training is not a onetime occurrence. It must become an ongoing continual improvement event.

Question Review Summary

After reviewing the survey, certain issues begin to come clear.

1. **Training** – Most companies do not give lubrication training the importance it deserves. Either there is no formal training, or "check the block" lubrication training is used. In other words, if asked, "Do you train your people in lubrication?" The answer would be "yes" but the training is not focused on providing changes to behavior or procedures that would improve the current state of

the lubrication program.

2. **Lubrication Procedures** – Part of a defined lubrication program is the existence of detailed lubrication procedures. If they have not been developed or, worse yet, they are not followed, you can have the best lubrication procedures in the world but they are useless. Management must ensure proper procedures are written and utilized.

3. **Importance to Reliability** – Many organizations do not see lubrication problems as a threat to reliability. Reliability ensures capacity, thus cost savings can be very significant compared to the cost of a defined, effective program.

Your lubrication program can be as complex as you like, but the recommendation and content of this text is focused on a simplified, effective method that works. It is further recommended that you, or someone in your organization, become lubrication knowledgeable beyond this text. The intent of this publication is not to make you a chemist or an oil expert, as that would be neither practical nor effective in your role as a lubrication practitioner. However, there are a few fundamentals that are important to understand in order to qualify actions taken for improving your current program.

Tribology is the science behind friction, lubrication, and wear of surfaces in relative motion, as well as the study and application of those principles. Our concern is with how friction occurs and how it can be reduced, through lubrication and its properties, in order to reduce wear.

Friction is the force resisting the relative motion of two surfaces in contact with each other. The by-products of friction are heat, wear, and sound. The two primary types of friction you are concerned with are:

- **Sliding Friction** – the friction caused by two objects rubbing against each other (gears).

- **Roller Resistance** – the forces that resist rolling along a surface caused by deformations in the object and/or surface (bearings).

Wear is the removal of material from a surface.

- **Adhesive Wear** – consists of scoring, galling, or seizing. Solid surfaces sliding over one another under pressure cause these effects. Surfaces become rough and deformed (scored/galled) and can weld together.

- **Abrasive Wear** – is generated by surfaces coming in contact with hard particles thus removing material. The particles can exist at the surface of a second material (two-body wear) or may be loose particles between two surfaces, i.e. lubrication contaminates.

- **Fretting Wear** – is the repetitive rubbing between two surfaces removing material from one or both surfaces. This is a common bearing defect identifying term of failure. If cracks occur this is known as fretting fatigue.

Lubrication is the process that provides a medium between surfaces moving relative to each other to carry the load, thus reducing friction which lessens heat and wear. A lubricant can be anything that reduces friction—oil, grease, water, air, powder, anything that would meet the definition. The problem is that not all lubricants will be effective when you consider application and operation context with the need to provide a cost effective component life cycle. The lubricant, in our case primarily oil and grease, when "ideal" keeps the surfaces from coming into contact with each other thus reducing friction. Your task is to keep the lubrication in, or as near as practical, an "ideal" state so that friction is kept at a minimum. Lubricants are also tasked with the removal of heat and wear particles and can protect surfaces from contaminates such as water.

Lubricating Oil, when applied to each of a component's surfaces, forms a thin film of oil as small as one micron (one millionth of a meter, or .0000394 of an inch) filling up the depressions and covering the projections. As long as the film of lubricant between the two surfaces keeps them from making contact with one another, no friction will occur. This condition is called fluid lubrication.

We must understand that this happens at a microscopic level. Viewing the un-lubricated surface under a microscope would reveal the surface to be uneven, full of pits, valleys, holes, as well as containing protruding peaks and edges. It is the adhesion of these deformities that causes friction. The film provided by effective lubrication keeps contact between the surfaces to a minimum. Effective lubrication is derived from considering load (pressures applied), speed (fast/slow), and the environment, atmospheric and internal (wet, hot, cold). Additives are used to assist in meeting the aforementioned requirements.

The oil forms in layers of globules, one layer adhering to each metal surface and any number of layers of globules in between. It should be noted that this depends on a satisfactory supply of oil to form a continuous film. Lack of oil after the rotation begins means that a lubricating film and wedge cannot be established, and the metal-to-metal contact will not be maintained, generating heat and eventually producing wear and failure.

Bearings are primarily oil lubricated. The oil film can be created by utilizing a pressurization system. This is called hydrostatic lubrication. The film can also be maintained by a "wedging" of lubricant developed by the rolling motion of the bearing itself. This is called hydrodynamic lubrication. Should the loads get too high or speeds too slow, the hydrodynamic action begins to fail and a condition referred to as boundary lubrication occurs.

Grease is made by adding a metallic soap to lubricating oil, effectively thickening it to the point that it turns into grease. The soap molecules in the grease cling together and have such a strong attraction with the oil molecules that it is very difficult to separate the soap and the oil. The soap molecules are "polar"—that is they carry an electric charge that causes them to be attracted to any electric field extending out a few molecule lengths from most metallic surfaces. This electrical attraction causes the formation of a minute layer of soap molecules on the metallic surfaces and these soap molecules attract molecules of oil. This attraction anchors a very thin film of grease (soap and oil) to the metallic surface.

Grease has a particular characteristic called directional fluidity. When moving in a bearing, the grease tends to "shear" into thin layers that move in the direction of rotation. As the shearing speed increases, the grease becomes easier to shear. This directional fluidity is encountered only in the direction of the shearing force, and the grease does not tend to run or be squeezed out of a bearing even though it is acting like a liquid.

Shearing stress reduces the apparent viscosity of the grease and falls rapidly until it approaches the viscosity of the oil used by its manufacture. The key to grease is to use the recommended grease specifications supplied by the manufacturer of the equipment, and the frequency of grease application based on a lubrication engineer's recommendation when available.

Hydrodynamic Lubrication occurs when the lubricant is able to support the load without external pressure. The lubricant film forms into a wedge-shaped channel generating a load-carrying pressure supporting the load. This form of lubrication is generally preferred because it is simple and dependable. The lubrication action improves as speed increases.

Hydrostatic Lubrication is the opposite of hydrodynamic in that pressure is applied in order to produce the film required to support the load. The main advantage of hydrostatic lubrication is that it can accommodate heavy loads at low speeds because it does not depend upon relative motion to maintain the lubrication film. The lubricant is supplied from a pump. It is preferred for many high-precision machine tools due to low deflection under certain load ranges. The disadvantage of hydrostatic lubrication is its high cost and complexity.

Boundary Lubrication occurs during startup and when heavy loads exist. At this point, the asperities (at a microscopic level the protruding surface peaks) come in contact with each opposing surface. Over 50%, perhaps even higher depending on the application, of wear comes at this point. As the equipment comes up to speed, lubrication separates the surfaces and this effect is lessened or eliminated. Anti-wear additives help to reduce these events even further. Also, higher viscosity lubricants can help but there is a balance (do not arbitrarily change your current viscosity). This is found mainly with slow-moving loads where the cost and expense of a hydrostatic system is not practical. Hinge bearings in aircraft landing gears, for example, do not move fast enough to develop hydrodynamic films, but hydrostatic systems would be too heavy, costly, and cumbersome. It is of the highest importance to have the right viscosity of oils and greases in the system to ensure proper lubrication.

Contamination of the lubricant can be caused by several unwanted occurrences. The introduction of foreign matter between metal surfaces is known as **particle contamination**. Foreign matter can destroy the lubricated surfaces by one of two actions. One action that occurs is the scratching of the metal surfaces inside a bearing (between rollers or balls and bearing race) causing friction and premature failure of the bearing. The second action occurs with loading a bearing (irregular load on the inside of the bearing presses against the bearing race) causing the bearing to heat up (the loss of lubricant on one side of a roller or ball creating heat) leading to premature failure of the bearing. The introduction of foreign matter between a set of gears can cause the same effect, as with bearings inside a gear reducer.

Note: 1 micron is one millionth of a meter (approximately .0000394 of an inch) whereas the smallest particle you can see with the unaided eye is 40 microns (or .0016 of an inch) – a grain of salt is about 100 microns. You can start to see the importance of keeping lubrication clean when you are trying to maintain the lubrication boundary between moving parts. Scratching of the surfaces (particles breaking the film) is the start of the fretting process and over time causes failure. Additional stresses are placed on the surfaces to overcome the lack of clearances. This all happens at a microscopic level and will evolve to eventual failure if not readily addressed, or better yet, avoided.

Improper lubricant type for application, over-greasing, mis-alignment, and other similar occurrences all produce heat and mechanically affect the bearing itself, degrading the lubricant's effectiveness.

Water is not an effective lubricant for mechanical devices. It is incapable of carrying any significant load – it is not compressible as is a typical oil based lubricant. As the oil film becomes a water film, the surfaces come in contact causing increased friction, wear, heat, etc. In the case of greases, when moisture contamination is unavoidable, you utilize grease with good water repelling additives. In oil lubrication, it is imperative to keep lubricants dry. Also recognize that water is a catalyst for rust and corrosion. Flaking rust produces particle contamination. Finally, be aware that in combustion engines, on a chemical level, water in the lubrication fluid is extremely harmful—you want to ensure dryness.

Although water ingression is common, it is also easily avoidable. Once detected, water ingression must be addressed immediately to avoid many of the indelible consequences.

There are several key properties that ensure the success of effective lubrication. The following is a list of those properties you will need to understand in order to become well-informed and diverse in the implementation and improvement of your lubrication program.

Viscosity is the most important property of lubrication oil/grease (Source Petroleum Handbook). Viscosity is a measure of a fluid's resistance to flow, and largely determines the suitability of an oil for any particular application. The best oil for a bearing is one with the right viscosity to maintain the "oil wedge" action efficiently, subject to conditions of speed, pressure and heat.

Oils with low viscosity rating are quite thin or light; while oils with high viscosity rating flow very slowly. The speed of a shaft and the clearance between shaft and bearing will determine the choice of oil. A slow turning shaft with relatively wide clearance can use heavy or high viscosity oil, while high speed shafts with close tolerance bearings require light or low viscosity oil. The viscosity of the oil should be based on the equipment manufacturer's specifications.

Viscosity Index (VI) and Viscosity Index Improvers are used to lessen the changes in viscosity as temperature increases (viscosity decreases) and decreases (viscosity increases). Viscosity Improvers, as with multi-grade motor oils, help lessen these changes. The higher the VI number the less change between temperatures. Typically, a VI of 100 is considered good. However, the VI of synthetics can exceed 400.

Additives, included in most oils, exist for three primary reasons:

1. To enhance existing base oil properties – Antioxidants, Corrosion Inhibitors, Antifoam Agents, Demulsifying Agents

2. To depress existing base oil properties – VI Improvers, Pour Point Depressants

3. To add new properties to a base oil – EP Additives, Detergents, Tackiness Agents

Oil aging is really the deletion of these additives, or contamination from the lack thereof. In determining what additives to use, remember that having more doesn't necessarily mean better, just more expensive.

Total Base Number (TBN) determines effectiveness in the control of acids formed during the aging process. Diesel engine applications will have high TBNs—10 or more. Typically, the oil can be scheduled for replacement when the TBN has reached 50% of its original value, at 75% it must be replaced immediately.

Total Acid Number (TAN) increases as oil quality decreases. This is one of the parameters to monitor in air compressor oil replacement. It is also applicable in combustible engines. When the TAN doubles, it's time to replace the oil.

Soot levels should remain below 2%, and not rise above 5%. This is a concern in combustible engines, and a primary parameter of interest in diesel engine applications.

Synthetic oils can be a viable alternative. They extend oil drains and are usually required in harsh applications such as air compressors. The biggest drawbacks to these oils are cost, and determining the correct synthetic replacement. Unless the environment, including the environment inside the machine, is of concern, you must justify the cost benefit of going synthetic. In selecting a synthetic, consult with the manufacturer.

Grease Soaps, like oils, come in a variety of types with various additives. Again, manufacturer recommendations must be followed unless careful analysis and consideration is taken. If brand names are used, identical or better brand specifications must be utilized. Most brand name specifications can be found on the internet. Lithium, Calcium and Polyurea greases are common in industry. It is important to know that not all greases are the same and not all are compatible with each other.

Included in the properties of the grease is the NLGI (National Lubricating Grease Institute) grade classification number (see figure below). Ranging from 000 – 6, it identifies the thickness, or texture, of the grease and its ability to hold the lubricant. Utilizing the incorrect grade will cause the lubricant to stay in the grease, causing poor lubrication, or fall out completely, causing little or no lubrication. Different NLGI grades should not be mixed.

NLGI Number	Thickness	Reference
00	Semi-fluid	Applesauce
0	Very soft	Mustard
1	Soft	Tomato paste
2	Moderately soft	Peanut butter

Hydraulic Fluids may not necessarily be considered lubricants. However, they can play an important role in your facility. There are only six things you have to do to ensure longevity of hydraulic fluids—keep the oil clean and dry, clean and dry, clean and dry. Simple oil analysis will tell you how successful you are.

Particle Contamination Levels are measured and compared by ISO 4406 standards. These standards can be purchased for about $60. However, there is plenty of information available on the internet. The following examples represent the minimum expected values for cleanliness at three particle levels. It is always best to ask the manufacturer for recommended targets.

- Journal Bearing = 17/15/12
- Roller Bearing and Hydraulics = 16/14/11
- Gearboxes = 17/15/12

Steps to Implement Effective Lubrication Practices

Having an understanding of lubrication fundamentals is important to understanding why you must implement effective lubrication practices. Lubrication practices are vital to maximizing reliability of your equipment.

In order to improve the reliability of your organization's lubrication program you must follow a few simple steps:

Assess Your Current State (Survey)

If you are unsure of performing an assessment on your own, ask your oil analysis lab manager what they can do to help. This assumes you have one—if you don't, then getting one is the first step in improving your program. Explain what you are trying to accomplish. You want to build a close working relationship. Promises of future work do not have to be made, but their willingness to help starts the desired partnership you require from all your support vendors. If this is not possible, you will have to attend a training class in order to be completely effective, but the following will get you started.

If lubrication samples have never been pulled on your systems, it is highly recommended you do so during this survey. This becomes your baseline and provides evidence of your improvement efforts. It is very important to communicate your current state and demonstrate how your efforts improve the overall condition of the systems.

Note: grease samples do not provide as much value as oil samples. We do not recommend performing grease samples unless there is a specific failure you need to address.

Always bring your camera when performing field assessments of any kind!

Create a Survey Form:

SURVEY FORM		
I. System/Equipment Tag Number	Asset ID	
II. System Description	Common plant name	• What is it called? • What does it do?
III. Lubrication Type	Multiple lines may be needed if the equipment has multiple lubricants.	• Grease • Lube Oil • Hydraulic • Etc.
IV. Lubrication Brand Name	If not readily known, you will need to find out, involve maintenance	
V. Viscosity	• Oil Grade (ISO VG – SAE – SSU) • Grease Type (Include NLGI number and soap type)	Obtain a copy of each product data sheet, available online. This will provide specific test results for comparison to application and/or other lubricants.
VI. Grease	Does the equipment have a tag identifying the proper grease type and maximum amount to apply?	The formula for determining re-lubrication grease amount is: $G = .005 \times D \times B$ where G = Grams of grease, D = bearing outside diameter in millimeters, and B = bearing width in mm. For nearly all bearing applications, the bearing should never be more than 1/3 full. Over greasing is a significant cause of bearing failure. For ounces and inches use .1 as the multiple. See appendix
	Does a color coded zerk grease cap exist identifying the required grease type?	In addition to identifying the proper grease, the cap lessens the possibility of injecting dirt into the bearing while greasing

	Is the bearing drain plug accessible and/or has the drain plug been replaced with a pressure release plug?	The Best Practice is to remove the drain plug, apply grease slowly while motor is running and allow excess to drain for about ½ hour. SAFETY FIRST—this is not always possible or convenient. Pressure release plugs help to avoid over greasing problems. Chances are if you cannot easily access the drain plug you are over greasing.
	Bearing number	If name plated, this helps in determining bearing size and re-lubrication volume. It's a good idea to have it documented.
	Are dedicated and calibrated grease guns by lube type utilized?	
VII. Lubrication Section, including Hydraulics	Is the oil type clearly labeled on the equipment?	Required
	Is the oil type color coded?	This is helpful if your makeup oil containers, used for refilling and topping off reservoirs, are also color coded—highly recommended.
	Reservoir Size	This is required to determine replacement value and oil analysis justification. If replacing the oil is less than the cost of extending oil replacements in the current schedule there may not be value in performing the analysis. However, proper identification of oil type is required. You also need to consider your history for catastrophic failure of similar equipment. If, in the past, wear analysis could have avoided an expensive repair, then analysis should be considered and may be cost effective.

	General condition of reservoir.	• Rusted? • Corroded? • Leaking? • Etc. If yes, this will need to be addressed.
	Is the reservoir completely sealed and vented through a desiccant breather?	It is extremely important to remove moisture and contaminants transported through the exchange of air during ventilation; desiccant breathers help to keep the oil clean and dry. Open vents are generally not acceptable, especially when particle and water contamination is a problem.
	Are there any leaks in the system?	You must develop the mindset that no leaks are acceptable. Small leaks become big leaks and if fluid can leak out, contaminates can be sucked in.
	Is there a sampling valve installed in a primary location—the spot were the most representative sample can be obtained—the return line just prior to the reservoir is typical.	Sampling at any other location (termed a secondary location) is only useful in isolating problems. In order to get a representative sample, it must be taken at the return line just prior to the reservoir. The primary sample location must be clearly tagged to ensure the correct location is used. Installation of Minimess valves is the preferred method for collecting oil samples. *Minimess Valves*

		In cases, such as engines, where this is not possible, oil will have to be drawn using a vacuum pump through the fill port or hatch. Care must be taken not to draw from the bottom—mid-sampling is ideal. Vacuum pumps can also be utilized in conjunction with the minimess valves. *Vacuum Pump*
		For oil bath applications, a pitot tube with a Minimess valve can be installed to ensure a representative sample. *Pitot Tube with Minimess Valve*
		Never utilize drain plugs/valves for samples. Everything heavy settles to the bottom, including water, and you will not get a representative of the system's fluid.
	Are there any dirty, rusted funnels? How about, containers that are not labeled?	If yes, throw them away.

	Are there any make up oil containers in the area?	Make up oil containers must be removed. This is a leading cause of contamination. Best Practice should mandate oil is retrieved from the supply room only when needed. The excess is returned or discarded.
VIII. Supply Room	Lubricants	
	Are oil drum/containers stored, at a minimum, in a covered area?	Ideally lubricants should be stored in an environmentally controlled building. If this is not option ensure drums are stored horizontally—if left vertical, there is a possibility of water being sucked into the drum during temperature changes. This also applies to drums taken to the field. Try to find a location away from traffic areas and avoid dusty locations. Keep containers loosely covered, drum covers/lids may also be helpful. (Never completely cover equipment in plastic wrap—moisture will develop.) All make up oil containers must be kept sealed in a relatively clean environment.
	Are bungholes tightly capped when not in use?	
	Are air breathers used during lubricant removal from supply drums?	This removes another source of contamination.
	Is everything clearly labeled?	Non-labeled containers must be disposed of.
	Are transfer procedures posted in the oil storage/supply transfer area?	There is less chance for someone to say "I didn't know" when procedures are posted.

	Are filtered transfer carts/systems used during the refilling and makeup oil process?	This is a must—anytime the oil is being transferred from the original supplier container to a clean makeup oil container or to a reservoir, the oil must be filtered to a level of 6 microns or less. Oils from suppliers are typically not delivered to this standard. "Clean" means microscopically clean not just visually clean. Damaging particles cannot be seen by the unaided eye. On that note, always use lint free rags when handling lubricants—fibers can also present problems. This may not be required with motor oils since the cleanliness required is not as tight as that for bearing lubrication or hydraulics.
	Is oil managed so that the older oil is utilized first?	Oil has a shelf life. You should always try to keep it fresh.
	Find a person who typically retrieves oil from the drum containers, ask him for 1 gallon of any type of oil, and observe. Regardless of his technique, simply watch, what you are looking for are possible future improvements.	If a solitary filter transfer unit is used for all transfers, you'll probably find it is not being flushed prior to filling the container. Ideally a filter unit exists for each type of oil—but this is not always practical.
	Grease	
	Are greases adequately stored?	Note observations.
	Find a technician. Pick a system and ask how he determines the type of grease to apply.	Hopefully, you won't get the response, "Whatever is in my grease gun." If you do, then you know you have some work to do.

	Are dedicated and color coded grease guns used?	The color should match the color of the zerk cap.
	Is each gun etched/ labeled in strokes per ounce/gram?	Procedures that state—"six strokes"—mean almost nothing since grease guns are not calibrated when manufactured. The amount must be in confirmed measures.

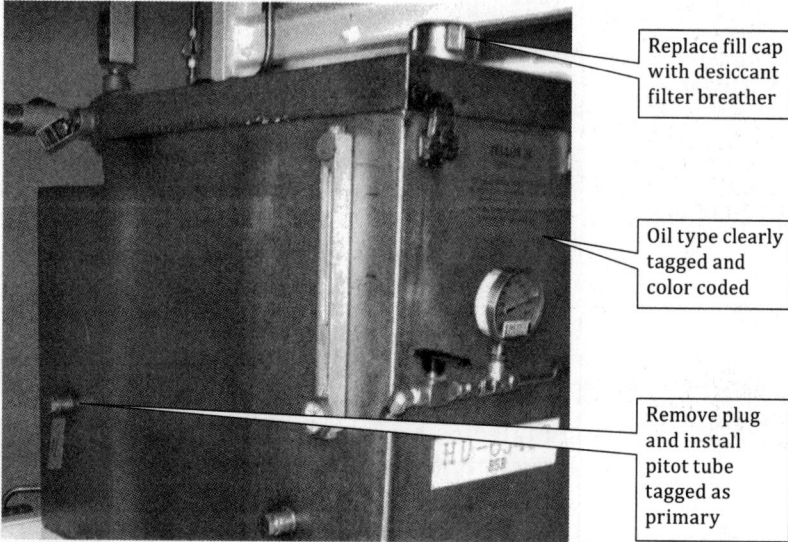

Replace fill cap with desiccant filter breather

Oil type clearly tagged and color coded

Remove plug and install pitot tube tagged as primary

Hydraulic System — Before Survey

Hydraulic System — After Survey

Oil Storage in Disarray...

Well, at least they are on their sides...

Oops... maybe not?

You'll probably note other deficiencies but this gives you a starting point. The items and devices mentioned can easily be found on the internet. When the survey is completed, place it in a spreadsheet. File pictures accordingly. Now it's time to develop a strategy. Consider the following questions:

- What can be done easily with minimal cost and effort?

- Where do you need maintenance and operations buy in?

- Clearly define estimated cost and time required for each improvement.

- What should you present to management?

- It is recommended you wait until the sample results are returned to present your findings.

- A cost saving. For example, you might show how oil drains can be extended with probable improved reliability. Be sure to include man hours saved by not replacing oil that is still good.

- A summarized plan for improvements. Progress should be measurable and include cost and man hours. Keep it simple but anticipate possible questions.

Justification and Improvement Strategy

Justification Example:

Let's say that for every hour your operation is down, your company notes that 25% of its total downtime is a result of lubrication problems. If the total downtime, over a particular timeframe, is 10% and 25% of the 10% is attributed to lubrication, then the total downtime attributed to lubrication, in comparison to total downtime, is 2.5%. If the projected total sales for a given year amount to $60,000,000 US Dollars then 2.5% (25% of the 10% total downtime) times $60,000,000 is $1,500,000 US Dollars in loss potential opportunity.

Encourage managers to substitute numbers as they see fit, either way, justification for improvements should be easily achieved. Remember, the first step in solving a problem is "knowing you have a problem" and the next step is "knowing how large the problem is".

Improvement Strategy

1. Train your maintenance/operations staff and anyone who handles oil or grease on lubrication best practices. Test them to validate the training has been effective.

   Train in knowledge areas such as:
   - Basic Lubrication Fundamentals
   - Basic Lubrication Practices
   - Contamination Control

   This should be done on-site and does not need to be

complex. Again, your lab personnel should be able to do this. If not, it is highly recommended you bring in an outside source for training. Hearing the message from an outsider may help address inner office culture issues, if they exist. You must attend each session to communicate the company's commitment to improvement. Keep in mind that one of two things happened to get you where you are: either employees were not instructed in proper methods or they have been allowed to perform poorly. In either case, it is not their fault. These training sessions are intended to help employees improve, to reduce cost and to relieve the frustration of unwanted repairs. Supervision, and even maintenance management, should also attend. Remember, "What's important to the boss is important to me."

The class should review the use of vacuum pumps, minimess valves and proper sampling techniques. Oil sample collection must follow standards to ensure induced contamination does not occur.

Include proper greasing practices, efforts taken thus far, as well as future improvements. This will have to be done before the new Preventive Maintenance procedures (PMs) are generated.

Advance training should be supplied to dedicated oilers and the Lubrication Program overseer.

2. In a lubrication procedure, define, including specifications, the proper way to lubricate all equipment.

Measure the performance of the lubrication program by providing metrics that track the program's performance.

• Start with a baseline before you implement this program. After implementation, measure on a routine basis.

- Trend the results and post without comment. After a few months, allow your maintenance staff to comment on the results. Ask them what they feel is working and what is not. Deficiencies are typically process problems, not people problems. People problems can be solved through training and enforcement of standards and processes.

"You cannot improve something that you cannot measure"
– Dr. Edward Deming

MINIMUM LUBRICATION SPECIFICATIONS	
Type of lubricant required	By brand or common name.
Amount of lubricant required	Obtain this information in the equipment manual or from the equipment manufacturer's technical support group.
	Bearing grease amounts can be calculated if the bearing sizes are known.
	Bearing size conversions can be obtained at SKF.com if you know the bearing replacement number, do not use a salesman.
Type of equipment required to perform the lubrication	Sample bottles and containers must be, at minimum, certified "CLEAN"
	Clean = max 100 particles >10 micron/ml
	Super Clean = max 10 particles > 10 micron/ml
	Ultra Clean = max 1 particle > 10 micron/ml
	Grease gun – calibrated in strokes per ounce
	Filter cart – with instructions
	Dedicated clean oil container for replacing oil in gear reducers or air compressors and other lubrication oils.
	Lint free rags when cleaning funnels for adding oil

Type of bearings in electric motors	Sealed bearings require no grease. It is recommend you mark motors with sealed bearings with a RED Tag warning, "DO NOT GREASE—SEALED BEARING" or better yet replace the zerk fitting (standard grease fitting) on the motor with a plug.
	Note: Be aware some motor manufacturers do install zerk fittings on motors with sealed bearings. This has to do with their production process where it is easier to have zerk fittings installed on all motors.
Procedures	
Should Include:	• Step-by- step how to perform proper lubrication.
	• Safety procedures that include both personnel safety and equipment safety.
	• Estimated labor hours required to perform the lubrication.
	• Technician sign off on PMs, and other routine inspections and tasks performed, must be a requirement.

3.   Report your successes. You want to provide management with progress reports as validation that the moneys they invested are paying off. At first, you will want to measure improvements made against your baseline. Also, track extended oil drains—using oil analysis to govern replacements rather than time. Follow manufacturer's specifications for frequency of oil change unless oil sampling analysis is performed. Take every opportunity to communicate successes.

• MTBF (Mean Time Between Failure) – The root cause of failures will have to be reviewed in order to identify the MTBF for lubrication. Compare then to now.

• Top 5 List of Lubrication Failures – Post the top 5 equipment problems that have failed because of lubrication issues. Track production losses (in dollars) and maintenance costs associated with each problem piece of equipment. Have the maintenance staff identify on the chart what action was taken to correct the problem. Communicate successes.

- Parts Cost – Track and trend bearing and gear reducer parts cost. You should see the trend in cost going down after a few months of implementing a successful program (discussed further in this text).

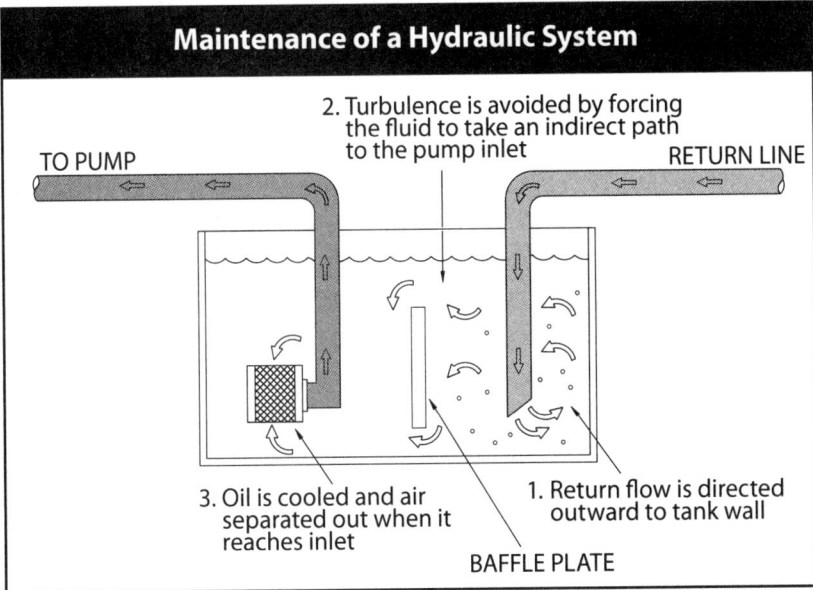

Maintenance of a Hydraulic System

TO PUMP

2. Turbulence is avoided by forcing the fluid to take an indirect path to the pump inlet

RETURN LINE

3. Oil is cooled and air separated out when it reaches inlet

1. Return flow is directed outward to tank wall

BAFFLE PLATE

Most companies spend a lot of money training their maintenance personnel to troubleshoot a hydraulic system. If instead you focus on preventing system failures then you can spend less time and money on troubleshooting. Normally, hydraulic system failures are expected, you can choose not to expect this as the norm. Spend the time and money to eliminate hydraulic failure rather than preparing for failure. In the 1980s, while working for Kendall Company, we changed our focus from reactive to proactive maintenance on our hydraulic systems to eliminate unscheduled hydraulic failure. We will talk about the right way to perform maintenance on a hydraulic system utilizing the "Maintenance Best Practices".

Lack of maintenance of hydraulic systems is the leading cause of component and system failure, yet most maintenance personnel don't understand proper maintenance techniques of a hydraulic system. Performing proper maintenance on a hydraulic system involves two areas of concern. The first area is Preventive Maintenance which is vital to the success of any maintenance program, whether in hydraulics or on any equipment in which we need reliability. The second area is corrective maintenance, which when not performed to standard, can cause additional hydraulic component failure.

Hydraulic System Preventive Maintenance

Preventive Maintenance of a hydraulic system is basic and simple and, if followed properly, can eliminate most hydraulic component failures. Preventive Maintenance is a discipline and must be followed as such in order to obtain results. We must view a PM program as performance oriented rather than activity oriented. Many organizations have good PM procedures but do not require maintenance personnel to follow them or hold them accountable for the proper execution of these procedures. In order to develop a preventive maintenance program for your system you must use the following steps.

1. Identify the system operating condition.

   • Does the system operate 24 hours a day, 7 days a week?

   • Does the system operate at maximum flow and pressure, 70% or better, during operation?

   • Is the system located in a dirty or hot environment?

2. What requirements does the Equipment Manufacturer state for Preventive Maintenance on the hydraulic system?

3. What requirements and operating parameters does the component manufacturer state concerning the hydraulic fluid International Organization for Standardization (ISO) particulates?

4. What requirements and operating parameters does the filter company state concerning their filter's ability to meet this requirement?

5. What equipment history is available to verify the above procedures for the hydraulic system?

As in all Preventive Maintenance Programs, you must write the required procedures for each PM Task. The steps or procedures must be accurate and understandable by all maintenance personnel from entry level to master.

Preventive Maintenance procedures must be a part of the PM Job Plan including:

- Tools or special equipment required for performing the task.

- Parts or material required for performing the procedure, with store room number.

- Safety precautions for the procedure.

- Environmental concerns or potential hazards.

1. ABC COMPANY

PREVENTIVE MAINTENANCE PROCEDURE

TASK DESCRIPTION: P.M. – Inspect hydraulic oil reserve tank level

EQUIPMENT NUMBER: 311111

FILE NUMBER: 09

FREQUENCY: 52

KEYWORK, QUALIFIER: Unit, Hydraulic (Dynamic Press)

SKILL/CRAFT: Production

PM TYPE: Inspection

SHUTDOWN REQUIRED: No

REFERENCE MANUAL/DWGS:
1. See operator manual F-378

REQUIRED TOOLS/MATERIALS:
1. Oil, Texaco Rando 68 SDK #400310
2. Flashlight
3. Oil Filter Pump

SAFETY PRECAUTIONS:
1. Observe plant and area specific safe work practices.

MAINTENANCE PROCEDURE:
1. Inspect hydraulic oil reserve tank level as follows:
   a) If equipped with sight glass, verify oil level at the full mark. Add oil as required.
   b) If not equipped with sight glass, remove fill plug/cap.
   c) Using flashlight, verify that oil is at proper level in tank. Add oil as required.
2. Record discrepancies or unacceptable conditions in comments.

PM Procedure Courtesy of Life Cycle Engineering, Inc.

Example of Preventive Maintenance Procedure

A list of Preventive Maintenance Tasks for a Hydraulic System could be (when applicable, include expected results):

1. Change the ("return" or "pressure") hydraulic filter.

2. Obtain a hydraulic fluid sample.

3. Filter hydraulic fluid.

4. Check hydraulic actuators.

5. Clean the inside of a hydraulic reservoir.

6. Clean the outside of a hydraulic reservoir.

7. Check and record hydraulic pressures.

8. Check and record pump flow.

9. Check hydraulic hoses, tubing and fittings.

10. Check and record voltage readings to proportional or servo valves.

11. Check and record vacuum on the suction side of the pump.

12. Check and record amperage on the main pump motor.

13. Check machine cycle time and record.

Preventive Maintenance is the core support that a hydraulic system must have in order to maximize component and life and to reduce system failure. Preventive Maintenance procedures that are properly written and followed will allow equipment to operate to its full potential and life cycle. Preventive Maintenance allows a maintenance department to control a hydraulic system rather than the system controlling the maintenance department. You must control your hydraulic system by telling it when you will perform maintenance on it and how much money you will spend on the maintenance for its system. Most companies allow the hydraulic system to control the maintenance, at a much higher cost.

In order to validate your preventive maintenance procedures you must have a good understanding and knowledge of "Best Maintenance Practices" for hydraulic systems. These "Best Practices" are outlined in the following pages:

BEST MAINTENANCE PRACTICES FOR HYDRAULIC SYSTEMS			
Component	Component Knowledge	Best Practices	Frequency
Hydraulic Fluid Filter	There are two types of filters on a hydraulic system. • Pressure Filter—comes in collapsible and non-collapsible types. Preferred filter is the non-collapsible type. • Return Filter—typically has a bypass, which will allow contaminated oil to bypass the filter before indicating the filter needs to be changed.	1. Clean the filter cover or housing with a cleaning agent and clean rags. 2. Remove the old filter with clean hands and install new filter into the filter housing or screw into place. CAUTION: NEVER allow your hand to touch a filter cartridge. Open the plastic bag and insert the filter without touching the filter with your hand.	Preferred: based on historical trending of oil samples. Least Preferred: Based on equipment manufacture's recommendations.
Reservoir Air Breather	The typical screen breather should not be used in a contaminated environment. A filtered air breather with a rating of 10 microns is preferred because of the introduction of contaminants into a hydraulic system. A desiccant breather filter is best because it will ensure the air exchanged is dry.	1. Remove and throw away the filter.	Preferred: Based on historical trending of oil samples. Least Preferred: Based on equipment manufacture's recommendations

Hydraulic Reservoir	A reservoir is used to: • Remove contamination. • Dissipate heat from the fluid. • Store a volume of oil.	1. Clean the outside of the reservoir to include the area under and around the reservoir. 2. Remove the oil by a filter pump into a clean container, which has not had other types of fluid in it before. 3. Clean the insides of the reservoir by opening the reservoir and cleaning the reservoir with a "Lint Free" rag. 4. Afterwards, spray clean hydraulic fluid into the reservoir and drain out of the system.	If any of the following conditions are met. A hydraulic pump fails. If the system has been opened for major work. If an oil analysis states excessive contamination
Hydraulic Pumps	Maintenance personnel need to know the type of pump they have in the system and determine how it operates in their system. Example: What is the flow and pressure of the pump during a given operating cycle? This information allows maintenance personnel to trend potential pump failures and troubleshoot a system problem quickly.	1. Check and record flow and pressure during specific operating cycles. 2. Review graphs of pressure and flow. 3. Check for excessive fluctuation of the hydraulic system (designate the fluctuation allowed).	Pressure checks: Preferred: Daily Least Preferred: Weekly Flow & Pressure checks: Preferred: Bi-weekly Least preferred: Monthly

Hydraulic Knowledge

Knowledge is power. This is definitely true in hydraulic maintenance. Many maintenance organizations do not know what their maintenance personnel should know. In an industrial maintenance organization, your hydraulic skills should be divided into two groups. One is the hydraulic troubleshooter, your experts in maintenance. They should comprise 10% or less of your maintenance workforce. The other 90% + should be your general hydraulic maintenance personnel. They are the personnel that provide the preventive maintenance expertise. These percentages are based on a company developing a true Preventive / Proactive maintenance approach to their hydraulic systems. Let's talk about the knowledge and skills required for each type of skill level.

Hydraulic Troubleshooter

Knowledge

- Mechanical Principles – force, work, rate, simple machines

- Math – basic math, complex math equations

- Hydraulic Components – application and function of all hydraulic system components

- Hydraulic Schematic Symbols – understanding of all symbols and their relationship to a hydraulic system

- Calculate – flow, pressure, and speed.

- Calculate – system filtration necessary to achieve the system's proper ISO particulate code

Skill

- Trace a hydraulic circuit to 100% proficiency.

- Set the pressure on a pressure compensated pump.

- Tune the voltage on an amplifier card.

- Null a servo valve.

- Troubleshoot a hydraulic system and utilize "Root Cause Failure Analysis".

- Replace any system component to manufacturer's specification.

- Develop a PM Program for a hydraulic system.

- Flush a hydraulic system after a major component failure.

General Hydraulic Maintenance Personnel

Knowledge

- Filters – function, application, installation techniques

- Reservoirs – function, application

- Basic hydraulic system operation

- Cleaning of hydraulic systems

- Hydraulic lubrication principles

- Proper PM techniques for hydraulics

Skills

- Change a hydraulic filter and other system components.

- Clean a hydraulic reservoir.

- Perform PM on a hydraulic system.

- Change a strainer on a hydraulic pump.

- Add filtered fluid to a hydraulic system.

- Identify potential problems on a hydraulic system.

- Change a hydraulic hose, fitting or tubing.

Measuring Hydraulic Improvement Success

In any program you must track success in order to receive support from management and maintenance personnel. You must also understand that any action will have a reaction, negative or positive. You know that successful maintenance programs will provide positive results but you must have a checks and balances system to ensure you are on track.

In order to measure success of a hydraulic maintenance program you must have a way of tracking success but first you need to establish a benchmark. A benchmark is a method by which you will establish certain key measurement tools that will tell you the current status of your hydraulic system and if you are succeeding in your maintenance program.

Before you begin the implementation of your new hydraulic maintenance program it would be helpful to identify and track the following information.

1. Track all downtime (in minutes) **daily** on the hydraulic system, answering these questions:

   - What component failed?

   - What was the cause of failure?

   - Was the problem resolved?

   - Could this failure have been prevented?

2. Track all costs **daily** associated with the downtime.

   - Parts and material cost

   - Labor cost

   - Production downtime cost

   - Any other cost that can be associated with a hydraulic system failure.

3. Track hydraulic system fluid analysis. Sample **monthly**.

   - Copper content

   - Silicon content

   - H_2O content

- Iron content

- ISO particulate count

- Fluid condition (viscosity, additives, and oxidation).

When the tracking process begins you need to trend the information that can be trended. This gives management the ability to identify trends that can lead to positive or negative consequences.

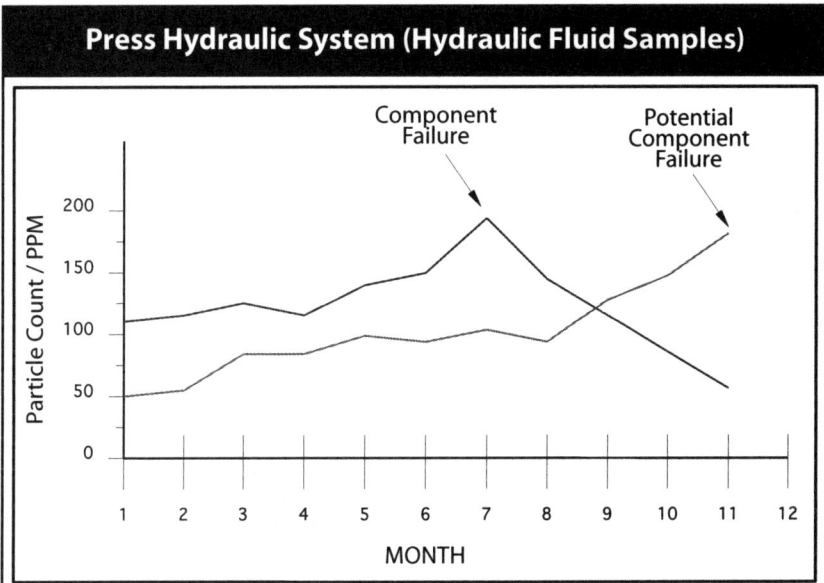

Press Hydraulic System (Hydraulic Fluid Samples)

In the example above, fluid analysis proved the need for better filtration. The addition of a 3-micron absolute return line filter to supplement the "kidney loop" filter solved the problem.

Many organizations don't know where to find the information they need for tracking and trending this information accurately. A good Computerized Maintenance Management System can track and trend most of this information for you.

Recommended Hydraulic Maintenance Modifications

Modifications to an existing hydraulic system need to be professionally executed. A modification to a hydraulic system in order to improve maintenance efficiency is important to a company's goal of maximum equipment reliability and reduced maintenance cost. The following recommendations can be modified to fit most of your lubrication needs.

1. Filtration Pump with Accessories:

Objective – to reduce contamination, introduced into an existing hydraulic system when adding new fluid and by the device used to add oil to the system, using a filter pump.

Hydraulic fluid from the distributor is usually not filtered to the requirements of an operating hydraulic system. This oil is usually strained to a mesh rating and not a micron rating. How clean is clean? Typically hydraulic fluid must be filtered to 10 microns absolute or less for most hydraulic systems, 25 microns is the size of a white blood cell, and 40 microns is the lower limit of visibility with the unaided eye.

Many maintenance organizations add hydraulic fluid to a system through a contaminated funnel and may even use a bucket that previously contained other types of fluids and lubricants without cleaning it.

Recommended equipment and parts (see figure below):

- Portable Filter Pump with a filter rating of 3 microns absolute.

- Quick disconnects that meet or exceed the flow rating of the Portable Filter Pump.

- A ¾" pipe long enough to reach the bottom of the hydraulic container your fluids are delivered in from your distributor.

- A 2" reducer bushing to ¾" npt to fit into the 55 gallon drum, if you receive your fluid by the drum. If you receive larger quantities, mount the filter buggy to the double wall "tote" tank supports.

- Reservoir vent screens should be replaced with 3 - 10 micron or desiccant filters and all openings around piping entering the reservoir should be sealed.

Filter Pumping Unit

Air Breather

55 Gallon Drum

10 Micron Filter

Portable Filter Pump

To Hydraulic
Reservoir

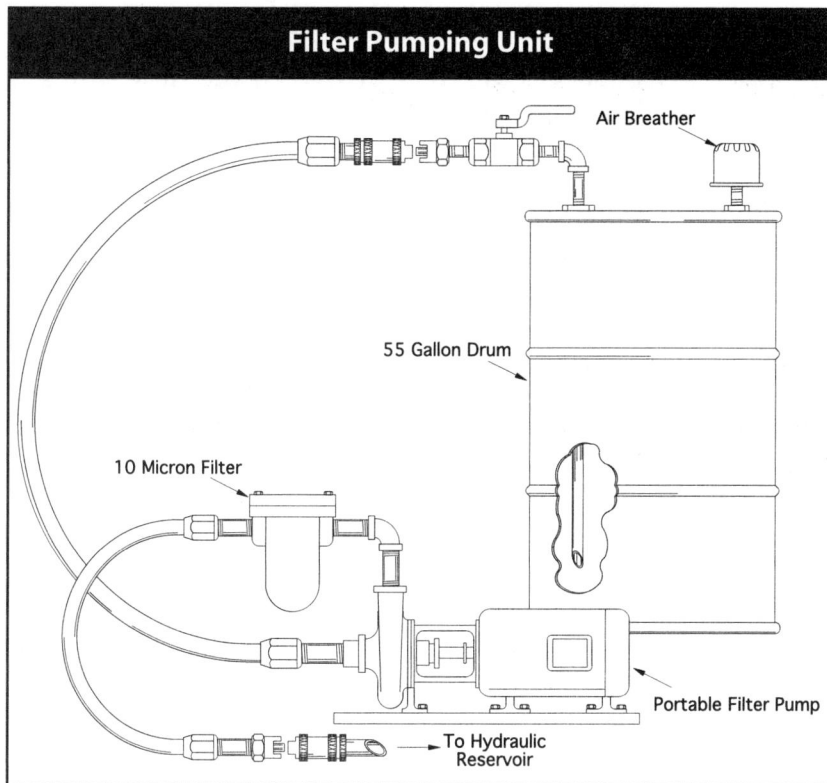

2. Modify the Hydraulic Reservoir:

Objective — to eliminate the introduction of contamination when oil is being added to the system or of contaminates being added through the air intake of the reservoir. A valve needs to be installed for oil sampling.

The air breather strainer should be replaced with a 10-micron filter if the hydraulic reservoir cycles. A quick disconnect should be installed on the bottom of the hydraulic unit and at the ¾ level point on the reservoir with valves to isolate the quick disconnects in case of failure. This allows the oil to be added from a filter pump as previously discussed and would allow for external filtering of the hydraulic reservoir oil if needed. Install a petcock valve on the front of the reservoir to be used for consistent oil sampling.

Recommended equipment and parts:

- Quick disconnects that meet or exceed the flow rating of the Portable Filter Pump.
- Two gate valves with pipe nipples.
- One 10 micron filter desiccant breather.

WARNING: Do not weld on a hydraulic reservoir to install the quick disconnects or air filter.

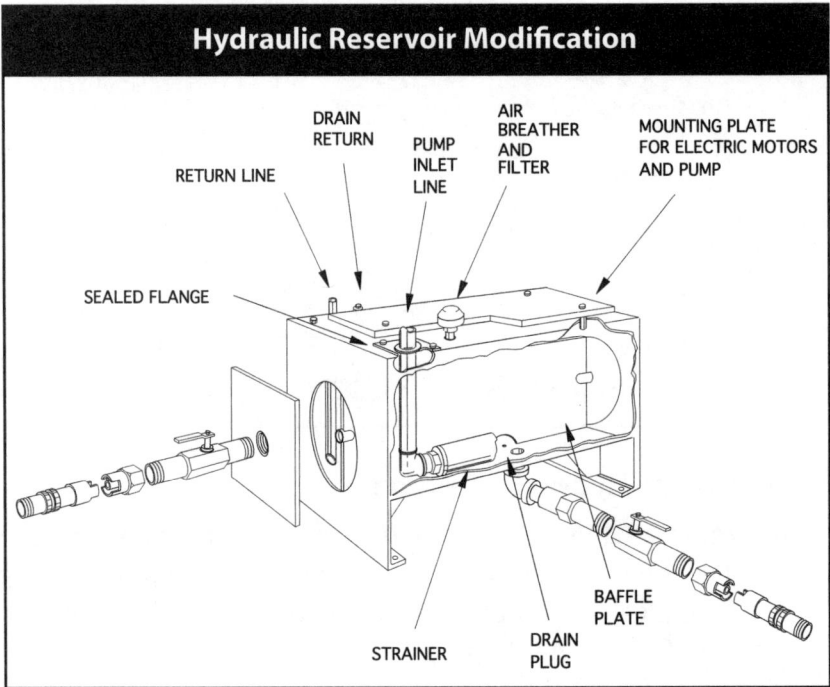

Hydraulic Reservoir Modification

Root Cause Failure Analysis

As in any proactive maintenance organization, you must perform Root Cause Failure Analysis in order to eliminate future component failures. Most maintenance problems or failures will repeat unless someone identifies what caused the failure and proactively eliminates it. A preferred method is to inspect and analyze all component failures. Identify the following:

- Component Name and model number.
- Location of component at the time of failure.

- Sequence or activity the system was operating at when the failure occurred.

- What caused the failure?

- How will the failure be prevented from happening again?

Failures are not caused by an unknown factor like "bad luck" or "it just happened" or "the manufacturer made a bad part". Most failures can be analyzed and steps taken to prevent their reoccurrence. Establishing teams to review each failure can pay off in major ways.

To summarize, maintenance of a hydraulic system is the first line of defense to prevent component failure and improve equipment reliability. Remember, discipline is the key to the success of any proactive maintenance program.

The following is by no means representative of everything you should know but rather covers those things that must be reviewed on each oil analysis report. Any decent lab will have these pointed out in the recommendations section of the report if they are outside acceptable limits.

1. Lubrication and Hydraulic Oils

   - Viscosity – to ensure it is correct and the right oil is in the system. Water and other contaminates can cause viscosity to vary. Oxidation will cause an increase in viscosity.

   - Cleanliness – must be within desired standards presented by manufacturer or industry standard. Reports of high particle contamination must have accompanying microscope slides – identifying type of contamination. If not within limits, circulate through your filter cart. It should be circulated at least 5 times to total volume or 4 hours, whichever is greater. Resample when complete to confirm success. Determine and eliminate ingression points. If the contamination is wear metals other troubleshooting may be required.

   - Water – must be dry. Standing water can be drained off. If the percentage is not too high it can be filtered out if you have water capturing capabilities in your filtration system. In some cases, the oil will need to be replaced – be sure to locate the points of ingression and fix them.

   - Ferrous – something containing ferrous (iron) materials is wearing or failing.

2. Engine Oils – a more thorough explanation can be found in the appendix—includes the previous in addition to:

   - Total Base Number (TBN) – when reduced to 50% of original it is time to schedule an oil change – at 75% it must be replaced immediately. This number is highest when the oil is new.

- Soot – schedule when at 2% and must rise above 5%. If it is excessive, or occurs quickly, piston ring(s) may be going bad, causing blow-by. Other elements of the report may support this occurrence. How's the fuel dilution?

- Metal element of the report (Spectroscopy) needs to be trended to ensure excessive wear is not occurring.

See sample of oil analysis report below.

Sample Oil Analysis Report

Ref Oil	Shell — Tellus — 68				
Sample Date	10/29/2008	5/27/2008	12/27/2007	9/25/2007	8/27/2007
Sample #	3824	3198	3784	3269	3191
Lab #	7111	3608	5424	4509	4104
Analyst	Jim D	Bill Rui	Keith M	Gary Gar	Gary Gar
Unit Usage (hrs)					
Oil Usage (hrs)					
Oil Added (gus)					
Wear	0	0	0	0	0
Ferrous Idx – Idx	0.0	0.0	0.0	0.0	0.0
LCont Ferrous – Idx	0	0	0	0	0
LCont NonFe – Idx	0	0	0	0	0
FW Idx – Idx					
Contamination	7	5	8	7	8
Contam Idx – Idx	0.0	0.0	0.0	.1	0.0
% Water – %	.005	.0183	.0157	.0016	.0178
% Water Soln – %					
LCont Droplet – Idx	0	0	0	0	0
Cnts >4 – pml	1,589	1,226	1,639	2,323	1,268
Cnts >6 – pml	145	186	523	430	417
Cnts >14 – pml	9	11	53	26	63
Cnts >22 – pml	2	4	10	7	21

Cnts >38 – pml	0	2	0	0	1
Cnts >70 – pml	0	0	0	0	0
ISO >4 – n/a	18	17	18	18	17
ISO >6 – n/a	14	15	16	16	16
ISO >14 – n/a	10	11	13	12	13

Chemistry	0	0	0	0	0
Chemical Idx – Idx	2.5	3.5	3.0	-8.3	3.4
Dielectric – Idx	2.15	2.24	2.24	2.13	2.24
DV Visc 40C – cSt	68.2	69.2	69.1	69.5	67.4
DV Visc %Chng – %	1.0	1.8	1.7	2.3	-.8

Let's take a look at why effective lubrication practices are important, and the steps necessary to implement them. You must first review the practices your company currently follows in regards to lubrication. If time based Preventive Maintenance Procedures (PMs) are currently being followed, the question may be, "Can the reliability of the equipment be monitored based on condition instead of time?" The chart below demonstrates this issue.

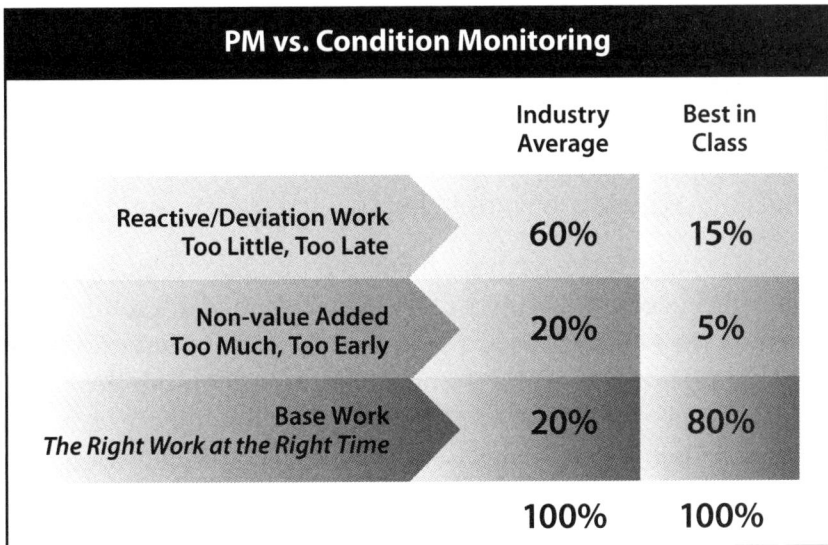

PM vs. Condition Monitoring		
	Industry Average	Best in Class
Reactive/Deviation Work Too Little, Too Late	60%	15%
Non-value Added Too Much, Too Early	20%	5%
Base Work The Right Work at the Right Time	20%	80%
	100%	100%

The chart above validates our survey in saying that reactive maintenance is the norm, i.e., too little, too late. If you are the "Best in Class" then you would monitor the condition of bearings based on sampling of oil or heat gain. If a conditioning monitoring process is used, what can an organization learn about the health of its assets and the current status of its lubricants? If you could monitor your assets' health based on condition monitoring, how would you manage that data? In order to have an effective condition monitoring program (oil analysis, amperage monitoring, vibration analysis, etc) you must manage the data with alarms set within your CMMS/

EAM to tell maintenance when an action is required. There are software programs sold on the market today that do just that.

Can bearings, lubricated with grease, be monitored based on amperage draw, vibration, etc? Begin, to think about different ways to lubricate your assets based on "condition" rather than "time". There will always be lubrication practices that will require "time based" PMs but begin to think about how to expand "condition based" monitoring at your facility. It is not recommended that you run right out and implement a condition based monitoring program without putting a lot of thought into it, but start thinking about how to change the way you are currently lubricating your equipment.

Ultra-sound greasing – Considered by some to be an improved method for greasing bearings over the typical scheduled greasing method. Adding grease only when needed, and to the required amount to restore to an acceptable condition, sounds like where you want to be, so what's the issue?

Studies (which the authors have been unable to locate) have been referenced indicating that an 8db rise in ultra-sound level indicates the bearing requires grease. In order to have a rise in ultra-sound level, there has to be some amount of film depletion (increased coefficient of friction), i.e. possible metal to metal contact. What is not clear is, at this level of lubrication, are detrimental affects occurring over the long-term? The depletion of lubrication occurs prior to the detection of heat or vibration since both require metal to metal contact to occur. So one could say ultra-sound is the lesser of two evils and is superior for incipient detection. Also, hundreds, if not thousands, of users of ultra-sound are reporting good results. The assumption can be made that it is effective.

We, however, do not like to work off of assumptions. Therefore, we are currently seeking more information on this subject. It is believed that someone has performed such studies, but we have yet to find them. Communications with bearings and ultra-sound companies have failed to produce adequate responses. Our recommendation, in regards to ultra-sound, is that if your current scheduled process is working then continue on, if not, ultra-sound may be something worth investigating further. You should also be able to determine if you are greasing too often (wasting man power), or too late (probable premature failure). Overall common sense should keep you from making things worse.

Some Lubrication-Related Failures

Following are some of the possible problems caused by lubrication which you may discover upon performing an analysis (the true root cause of the failure):

BEARINGS	
Problem Found	**Root Cause**
1. Bearing failure due to contamination of the grease with dirt, dust, or silicone.	1a. Someone failing to wipe a grease fitting, or the end of the grease gun nozzle, clean.
	1b. Seal not holding due to over-lubrication.
2. Bearing failure due to lubricant not providing barrier to prevent metal to metal contact.	2a. Wrong grease/oil.
	2b. Heat reduced viscosity from outside temperature rise beyond range of lubricant.
	2c. Mixing of incompatible greases.
GEAR REDUCERS	
Problem Found	**Root Cause**
1. Failed bearings and damaged gear teeth due to contamination reducing interference between gears, thus loading bearings.	1a. Gear oil added to the gearbox through a dirty funnel, container, or bucket.
	1b. Seal not holding due to over-lubrication.
2. Failed bearings due to contamination of the lubricant in the bearing with dirt, dust or silicone.	2a. Seal leaking due to over pressurization of gearbox—caused by blocked air intake on gear reducer.
	1a. Someone failing to wipe a grease fitting, or the end of the grease gun nozzle, clean.

62

ELECTRIC MOTORS	
Problem Found	**Root Cause**
1. Bearing failure due to contamination of the grease with dirt, dust or silicone.	1a. Someone failing to wipe a grease fitting, or the end of the grease gun nozzle, clean.
	1b. Seal not holding due to over-lubrication
2. Windings failed because of grease build up inside the motor.	2a. Relief plug not removed from bottom of motor before grease is introduced into the zerk fitting on the motor.
	2b. Sealed bearings in motor that require no greasing—grease cannot enter into the bearing because of the seal.
	2a. Wrong grease/oil.

Other Considerations of Failures

In many cases, lubrication is blamed for bearing failures when other causes may actually be the root cause. You must look for the true root cause of any failure before coming to a conclusion. Otherwise, you end up treating a symptom and not the problem. Some examples of problems which can be attributed to lubrication failures are:

a. Storage of Bearings: If bearings are stored improperly then premature failure can result. Lubrication failure is usually blamed instead of the storage problem. If bearings are allowed to lay open on a storeroom, are stored in an environment where the storage area has vibration, or if large bearings are not rotated on a scheduled basis, then premature failure will occur. The same holds true for your motor spares—all must be stored properly and rotated monthly.

b. Installation of Bearings: If bearings are installed improperly then premature failure will occur. Again, many times lubrication problems are blamed. Installation of bearings must be done in a controlled manner where "best installation practices" are followed. For example: never handle bearings with a bare hand, never rotate a bearing that does not have lubrication on it, and always heat the bearing to bearing manufacturer's specifications before installing to an interference fit.

c. Installation of Gear Reducers: You must follow the manufacturer's recommendations when installing a new or rebuilt gear reducer. Most gear reducer manufacturers will tell you, for example, that the gear reducer must have the oil changed within 24 - 48 hours of operation. This process allows all foreign matter that may be in the gear reducer to be removed. Following this process, as a maintenance supervisor in the 1980s, led to never having a gear reducer fail after installation—these gear reducers operated without problems for many years.

d. Alignment: Proper precision alignment is critical to equipment longevity. All machines are to be aligned to recommended tolerances. You must also consider thermal growth and operational displacement for proper alignment results. Machines that are suspect should have alignment confirmed. After running to temperature for some time, immediately perform an alignment test. You may find that the results from cold to hot are very different.

f. Bearing Isolator Seals: When contamination with moisture or other contaminates is prevalent at the drive in of the motor, consider installing a bearing isolator on your next repair or purchase. There are several available. Your motor repair shop should be able to help you.

g. Break-in Oil Drains: Approximately 50 hours after a new or repaired piece of equipment is placed online, drain and flush the system. This will aid in the removal of break in, building, and repair contaminates. If this is not feasible, perhaps due to large quantities and the associated cost, adding a filter circulation system is acceptable. If the equipment arrives with oil in it, pull a sample immediately to confirm the oil is acceptable for use. Drain and flush as described above.

h. Over Greasing: Applying too much grease by improper draining during greasing, applying grease too quickly, in quantities exceeding recommendations during re-greasing, or too frequently, can be as bad, if not worst, as poor lubrication. When over-greased roller bearings slide instead of roll, bearing fits are stressed and excessive heat is produced, all detrimental to the reliability of the bearing.

i. Mixing Greases: Assuming the general properties are within desirable limits for the application, mixing of the grease bases will cause either the soap to harden, reducing its ability to properly lubricate, or, more likely, the oil will quickly fall out of the base resulting in lack of lubrication. Be cautious of indications showing them to be somewhat compatible. Although fall out of the oil doesn't happen as quickly as it typically would, it will fall out none the less. The only effective way to ensure compatibility is to have the greases tested in a lab.

Thickener or Soap Type	Aluminum Complex	Barium Complex	Calcium Stearate	Calcium 12-Hydroxy	Calcium Complex	Calcium Sulfonate Complex	Clay (non-soap)	Lithium Stearate	Lithium 12-Hydroxy	Lithium Complex	Polyurea (conven. 1st gen.)	Polyurea (LUB – L/M type)
Aluminum Complex	•	|	|	C	|	N	|	|	|	C	|	C
Barium Complex	|	•	|	C	|	C	|	|	|	|	|	N
Calcium Stearate	|	|	•	C	|	C	C	C	N	C	|	C
Calcium 12-Hydroxy	C	C	C	•	N	N	C	C	C	C	|	C
Calcium Complex	|	|	|	N	•	|	|	|	|	C	C	C
Calcium Sulfonate Complex	N	C	C	N	|	•	|	N	N	C	|	C
Clay (non-soap)	|	|	C	C	|	|	•	|	|	|	|	N
Lithium Stearate	|	|	C	C	|	N	|	•	C	C	|	C
Lithium 12-Hydroxy	|	|	N	C	|	N	|	C	•	C	|	C
Lithium Complex	C	|	C	C	C	C	|	C	C	•	|	C
Polyurea (conven. 1st gen.)	|	|	|	|	C	|	|	|	|	|	•	C
Polyurea (LUB – L/M type)	C	N	C	C	C	C	N	C	C	C	C	•

Above is a typical compatibility chart (several are available on the internet).

j. Repair Shops: It is vital that you get very close to your repair shops. These shops provide a great opportunity to improve your current state. They must recognize that the expectation is for them to become a partner in your effort to improve. Repair specifications are also highly recommended because there are several ways to repair equipment—to your standards or every other way. DO NOT LET the repair shop create your specifications—instead, if you do not feel comfortable writing them yourself, hire a consultant. It will be some of the best money you have ever spent.

When visiting the repair shops to witness equipment operations, utilize your time there as learning and training opportunities. Ask them to demonstrate and explain a part of their repair process. It could be the Disassembly and Initial inspection process. What does the inspector look for? How is it documented in your repair reports? Watching equipment operate at the shop, after it's been repaired, provides almost zero value. The value is in the opportunity to learn techniques you can bring back to the field to avoid future visits to the repair shop. Should you feel as though the repair shop is not meeting your needs, move on. You've already wasted too much time with them.

k. New Purchase Standards: Development of what is required for new purchases is a must. It happens over and over again. New equipment comes into the plant under the assumption it has been designed and built to Best Practices and instead you end up with substandard equipment with minimal reliability capabilities. To refit these in the field is far more expensive than doing it right in the first place. These results are not the vendor's fault, it is yours. You must be clear in your expectations and hold the vendor to them. Without standards, they will continue to keep the bid cost low—and the reliability low, making production cost high. This would seem to be self-evident and, yet, it happens every day.

Determining Re-greasing Quantity and Timing of Bearings

When manufacturing recommendations are not readily accessible, the following Rule of Thumb charts can be used to determine the frequency and amount of grease required for re-greasing. However, it is always recommended to check manufacturing data first, calculate volume based on bearing size (G=.005 x D x B) then see Rule of Thumb charts. Adjustments can be made based on experience *(see appendix for more)*.

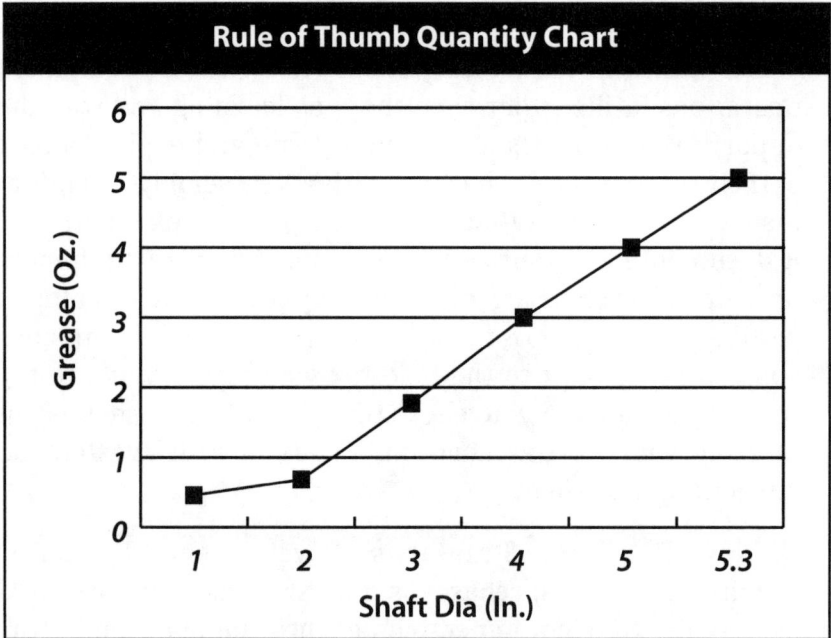

Rule of Thumb Quantity Chart

Rule of Thumb Frequency Chart

Relubrication intervals at 158° F (70° C)

Hours

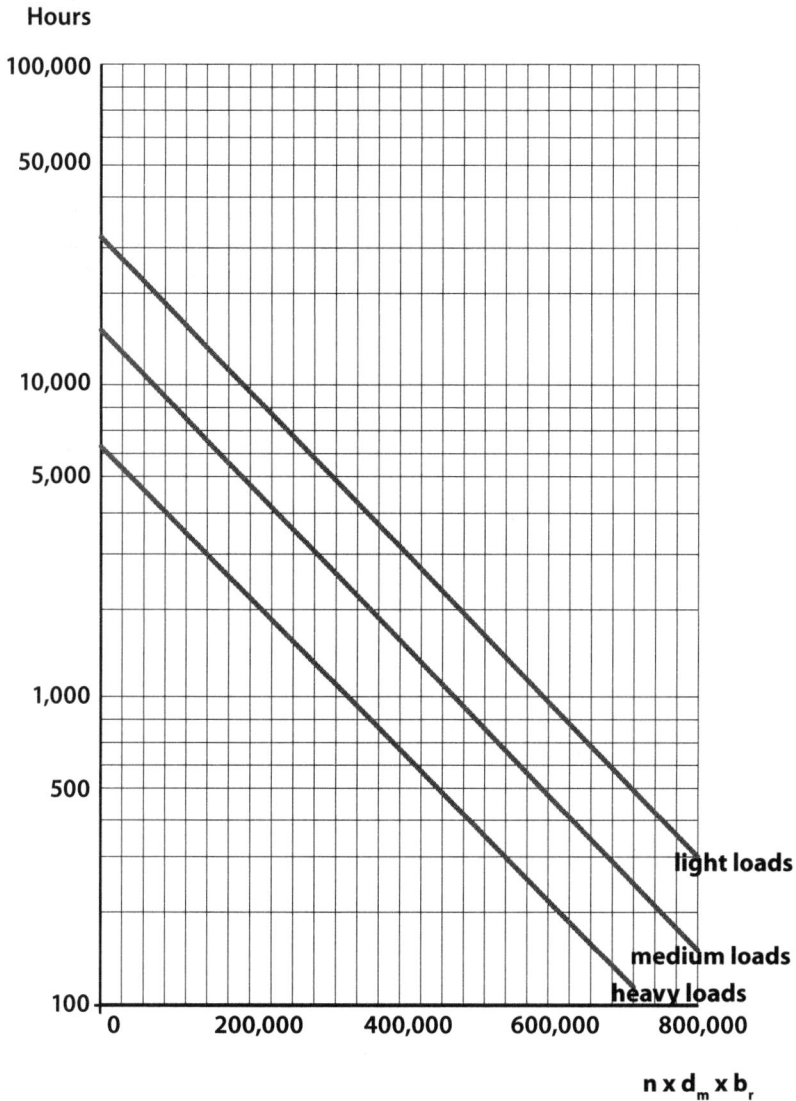

100,000

50,000

10,000

5,000

1,000

500

100

0   200,000   400,000   600,000   800,000

light loads

medium loads

heavy loads

$n \times d_m \times b_r$

Measuring Cleanliness

"Cleanliness is next to Godliness", everyone's heard that saying. It also holds true in the world of maintenance, particularly in lubrication. One thing to look at in ensuring cleanliness is particle counting. Particles can be any size, with some more detrimental than others, depending on the application. They consist of dirt, dust, sand, scale, rust, metals, and fibers, basically anything that is not natural to the lubricant. You do not want anything to break the film barrier. It's what keeps your moving surfaces separate. Particles in the film medium will break the film causing imperfection in the surfaces. These imperfections cause further lubrication film breakdown through vibration and, in some cases, heat. If left unattended, they worsen as time passes, until catastrophic failure is reached. "Keep it Clean, Dry, Cool" is the motto for maintenance and reliability.

Light Blockage Analysis is the process used to determine the amount of particles in a sample. Basically, 5 ml of fluid is placed in an analyzer (Optical Particle Counter) and a laser beam is shot through the fluid onto a detector. The detector is able to determine the amount and size of the particles in the fluid as the light passes through. Any particles in the fluid block the beam causing shadows on the detector. Water (and air bubbles) interfere with the analyzer's capability to work properly and will be discussed later. Dark oils, such as engine motor oil, which have been in service for some time, also interfere with the analyzer.

To ensure everyone is speaking to the same thing, reference standard ISO 4406 for the guidelines and scale reference. The analyzer determines the actual particle count per milliliter.

Oil Analysis Report

Cnts >4 – pml	1,589	1,226	1,639	2,323	1,268
Cnts >6 – pml	145	186	523	430	417
Cnts >14 – pml	9	11	53	26	63
Cnts >22 – pml	2	4	10	7	21
Cnts >38 – pml	0	2	0	0	1
Cnts >70 – pml	0	0	0	0	0
ISO >4 – n/a	18	17	18	18	17
ISO >6 – n/a	14	15	16	16	16
ISO >14 – n/a	10	11	13	12	13

Noting the oil analysis report above, you can identify how many particles are in the sample, compare it to previous analyses (each column represents a different date of oil sampling on the same unit), and determine whether it is within industry or manufacturers' standards. Industry determines cleanliness by examining the amount of particles <4 microns >6 microns/and >14 microns. Noting the figures above, you would say that the cleanliness of this oil is 18/14/10. Another way to determine the amount of particle counts (Cnts) is >4 is 1,589, >6 is 145 and >14 is 9. Utilizing the table below you can determine again that the ISO reading is 18/14/10.

ISO Table

ISO Code	Particle Counts > including	
10	5	10
11	10	20
12	20	40
13	40	80
14	80	160
15	160	320
16	320	640
17	640	1300
18	1300	2500
19	2500	5000
20	5000	10000
21	10000	20000
22	20000	40000
23	40000	80000
24	80000	160000
1–9 Codes are not shown. If you get those readings the oil is clean.		

For simplicity, the entire code table (codes 1-9) is not shown. In actuality, if your ISO is 10 or lower, your fluid is clean. In other words, the exact number of particles is not as important as recognizing and understanding the cleanliness codes.

As a general guide, you can look at the string of code to

determine, at a glance, whether or not there are concerns. For example, regardless of application, a code like 20/18/15 would be high and would warrant a better understanding of the application. In an engine, this may be acceptable. A reading of 17/15/12 is the midrange, and typical for many applications. 15/13/11 is a good reading for hydraulics which typically require the utmost attention to cleanliness. There are several application cleanliness charts available but no inclusive standard, only references. The best practice is to check with the equipment manufacturer for their recommendation. If this is not achievable, you'll have to determine what is achievable based on filter specification, protection from contaminate ingression and your application. Obviously this must be balanced against cost.

Remember cleaner is better but you must be practical with your intended outcome. You should ensure there is a problem before you take steps to correct it. Making corrections to improve cleanliness will take time, money and dedication. Don't waste maintenance time addressing problems that don't exist.

Referencing the Oil Analysis report from right to left, you can see that our quarterly samples have been between 18/16/12 to as clean as 17/15/11. What action was taken when it went from 17/16/13 to 18/16/12 —nothing! One step in code readings doesn't warrant action. Even after two steps, you may want to think about it. If you determine to take action, the first step is to demand a micro-slide of the sample from your lab. This will help to identify the problem. It is very important to utilize cleanliness practices when taking lubrication samples. Remember, in dealing with lubrication samples, you are working with particles you cannot see that may well be guiding future work. If you are suspicious of the sample, have maintenance pull another sample for retesting/conformation. Explain what was found and ensure proper practices are used. Rush the sample for retesting—have maintenance pull it right away, have shipping send it out ASAP and contact the lab to let them know you are sending an emergency sample for retesting.

Obviously, water in the sample doesn't have to be tested or

retested (see figure below). One concern worth investigating would be to find out if it was raining during the sampling. Was the sample contaminated by the rain? Was it pulled from a bottom drain? Ask the tech if he noticed free water or a milky appearance to the oil when sampling. You should know that when these conditions exist, they require immediate attention. Save your money and don't send these samples out. You need to find where the water is getting in, seal it, and remove what water is there. Depending on the condition of the oil, you may not have to replace it. Also, do not be too quick to assume it is from condensation and nothing can be done about it. Although this is a possibility, exhaust all other possible sources of ingression first. If you are not using desiccant breathers, you may find them a worthwhile consideration, desiccants will eliminate these occurrences. As stated previously, Light Blockage doesn't work well if there is water in the sample. You'll often get readings like 24/23/22 that really stick out. When such readings occur, the first thing to do is look at your water content.

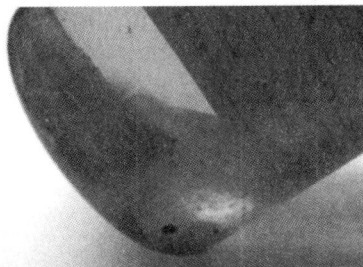

Free Water and Particulates

Emulsified Water (Milky)

If someone tells you that you have bacteria in your fuel reservoir, and you find no trace of water in the reservoir or in the floor location of the tank—you do not have bacteria. You cannot have bacteria without water. Something else is going on. Should someone recommend you add a bactericide to protect from bacterial growth, and you are sure you do not have a water ingression problem, remember that you cannot have bacteria without water. On the other hand, if you have a bacteria problem, you do have a water ingression problem. To solve the problem, find the source of the water.

Measuring Results

One way to ensure you remain within cleanliness standards is to develop a chart showing your initial baseline results compared to your most recent analysis results. In the chart, the diamond-shaped symbol represents initial readings and the square-shaped symbol the most current results.

IX
CONCLUSION

It may seem like a daunting task to align desired outcomes with current capabilities. Taking a simple approach is the best way to achieve long-term goals. Don't let the critics hinder your longing for improved reliability or your determination for achieving success. You might hear comments that indicate you are missing things that could be important, and that could be right. However, what if you don't do anything and the status quo remains the same. Are you really accomplishing anything? Even now, you are probably missing something. Let's face it, you aren't going to become a chemist, and maybe not even a lubrication expert, that doesn't mean you can't implement sensible lubrication practices or understand oil analysis to the level of ensuring asset health and reliability.

The content of this text is intended to get you started. It presents practical, sound, and proven approaches to improving equipment lubrication. Being serious about implementing and following these objectives will drive you and your program to maturity. As always, you are encouraged to seek out further knowledge. The internet is wonderful for finding information on standards and practices.

Get and give training. Formal training is important but not your only choice. Several really good formal training opportunities are available but don't forget to utilize the knowledge of your suppliers, vendors and even the things you have learned on your own. Often, providing a one hour lunch-and-learn session can be more productive than a four day offsite-course. Develop partnerships with vendors and suppliers that can further your goals. Eliminate those who are only interested in what you can do for them. Have maintenance (those involved with the aspects of lubrication) understand the objectives of improved lubrication practices. Present the knowledge in such a way that they won't feel as though they have been doing anything wrong, rather that this may be a better way of doing things. Ask your maintenance people for their help—you need them in order to be successful.

And lastly, but most importantly, never be satisfied with your current situation unless you are achieving your desired outcomes routinely. Continual Improvement should always be your goal and your motto. Often the limiting paradigm for many people is how to get started. Hopefully, this paradigm no longer exists for you!

APPENDIX

Free Analysis

Some oil manufacturers offer free analysis (Sullube air compressor oil). It is difficult to beat a free intuitive analysis. Discuss this with your equipment and oil supply vendor.

Dow

Lubricant Technology Center

The Dow Chemical Company
2301 Brazosport Blvd.
Freeport, TX 77541 USA
(979) 238-9992 Fax: (979) 238-6068

November 4, 2008

Contact Person
Address   Phone ###

Compressor Analytical Lubricant Report

Customer: T F Air Compressor	**Viscosity**..........	246 SUS
Sample #: 11XXXX **Fluid Type:** Sullube	**Acidity**	5.10 pH
Sampled: 10/28/2008 **Fluid Hours:** (1000)	**Total Acid No.** ....2.62 mg KOH/g	
Logged: 10/30/2008 **Unit Hours:** (24535)	**Methanol Insolubles**..	0%

Serial No.: _____

Model No.: _____

Customer Comments & Requests:
Equipment Number/Tag
Work Order # – PO Number

Explanations:

Viscosity	The viscosity trend should be watched, as it is somewhat higher than normal.
pH	The pH of this sample is marginal.
Total Acid No.	Very high. The machine should be flushed and changed.
Methanol Insolubles	No significant level of contamination was detected.

Suggestions:
This machine should be drained, flushed and refilled immediately due to a very high total acid number (TAN).

Oil Analysis Results

Below is a summary sheet for oil analysis results for a 7200 hp Caterpillar Engine. If you develop something similar, you will find it useful not only for yourself, but for communicating with others as well.

Diesel Engine Oil Analysis Report Explained				
Rotella 15W40 (*text in italics taken directly from CAT literature*)				
WEAR METALS		**SPECTRO CHEMICAL ANALYSIS**		
The oil sample is ionized in a control chamber. The light from this burning process is separated by a diffraction grating (much like a prism). Each element emits its own characteristic wavelength of light (energy). Photomultiplier tubes are positioned to collect this light from the specific metals. With the aid of a computer, the intensity of light is compared to a standard and converted to parts per million. Drawback—particle sizes in excess of 8 microns could be missed as part of the analysis. To avoid this D.R. Ferrography is used to verify particle sizes. ISO Cleanliness is a back up reading.				
Reference Sample Results			**ALERT**	**ALARM**	**Possible Causes for Elevated Readings**
Iron Fe	ppm	2	30	80	Cylinder walls/liners, valves, shafts, pistons, crankcase
Chromium Cr	ppm	0	7	10	Piston Rings, anti-friction bearings, shafts, blow-by. Abnormal operating temperature-dirt, restricted air induction system.
Molybdenum Mo	ppm	0		10	Mechanical friction modifier. In oil from blow-by.
Aluminum Al	ppm	1	14	100	Bearing wear, critical, small levels require immediate attention.
Copper Cu	ppm	0	30	100	Bearings, bushings, thrust washers, may be high if application has a copper oil cooler
Lead Pb	ppm	0	30	100	Bearings
Tin Sn	ppm	0	30	100	Bearings, plating.
Silver Ag	ppm	0	>1	25	Silver solder, wrist pin bushings (EMD).

Nickel Ni	ppm	0	4		100	Shafts, valves
Vanadium V	ppm	0	10		75	By-products of heavy fuel oil and occasionally a wear metal. When from fuel, during combustion vanadium produces corrosive salts. These salts are not harmful if kept below their 480^{0}C (900^{0}F) melting point. Exhaust valves are most vulnerable, but turbochargers can also be affected.
Titanium Ti	ppm	0	30		100	Contained in some alloys.
Manganese Mn	ppm	0				Contained in some new oils as an additive.
Cadmium Cd	ppm	0				Contained in some new oils as an additive.
Combination Silicon, Chromium, Iron						Dirt entry through the induction system, possibly causing ring and liner wear
Combination Silicon, Iron, Lead, Aluminum						Dirt entry through the lower portion of the engine, possibly causing shaft and bearing wear.
CONTAMINANT METALS						
Silicon Si	ppm		6	14		Airborne dirt may be high due to silicon containing additives, Air Induction System Filters, Turbocharger Breathers.
Sodium Na	ppm		1	200	400	An agent of engine coolant, ingression—causes oil to thicken and become sludgy, leading to piston sticking and filters plugging.
Boron B	ppm		1	200	400	An agent of engine coolant, ingression

ADDITIVE METALS					
Magnesium Mg	ppm	14			Detergent (Protects from varnish, sludge, gum buildup)
Calcium Ca	ppm	4304			Detergent (Protects from varnish, sludge, gum buildup)
Barium Ba	ppm	0		10	Rust & Corrosion Inhibitor
Phosphorus P	ppm	1345			Anti-wear Component
Zinc Zn		1370			Anti-wear Component
NON-METALLIC CONTAM.					
Water	% vol	Alarm Trace Nil		>.5% <.5% <.2%	Water can destroy bearings and other components quickly. Nil is the preferred reading. *Mostly caused by condensation in the crankcase, more serious concentrations from cooling system. Water passing through mating surfaces creates "hot spots" which when hot enough, cause miniature steam "explosions." these explosions cause metals to fracture. (Heat generates oxidation...)* Set Carl Fisher <.2%)
Solids	% vol	< 0.1			(See below)

Total solids are solids and semi-solid particulates contained in the oil sample. These are generally excessive oxidation resins, and/or combustion by-products (carbon). Typical sources of oxidation resins are high operating temperatures and/or extended oil drain intervals. Blow-by products can be caused by poor mechanical efficiency. Items such as incorrect injector and ignition valve timing, air to fuel ratio, or abnormal wear in piston ring and cylinder regions cause excessive blow-by.

Fuel	% vol	< 2.0	>=2.0	>4	Identifies possible piston ring failure, leaking injectors, seals, fuel fittings, pumps. Fuel dilution refers to raw or cooked fuel that has contaminated the crankcase oil, generally indicative of mechanical malfunction, leakage or abnormal operating conditions.
LUBE DATA	Depending on where you started, virgin oil with 15 to 30 minutes runtime, the viscosity's maximum allowable limit for change should be 15% according to Shell's representative for Rotella. Note that beginning with the specification reading of 15.7 (Rotella Spec) the 15% increase equals to an 18cSt and will take it outside of the SAE 40 Grade which is 12.3 to 16.5 cSt at 100°C. Again the Rotella rep stated this is satisfactory because of the starting point. ***Short version – You should never go beyond a viscosity reading of 18 cSt at 100°C. (AGAIN it is important to pull the baseline when oil is replaced as this is the starting viscosity point to measure against.)				
Viscosity at 100° C	cSt	15.2	10%	15%	Look for change. 20% plus, 10% minus. Should not increase more than 3 cSt Test Method - ASTM D445
Total Acid Number (TAN)	Units	>3.5	5	5	When oil degrades it generally becomes more acidic and corrosive. TAN is one key element used to determine when oil requires replacement. The following influences TAN: Temp., Moisture, Aeration, Particles (especially metal wear particles.) Alarm at double the original base reading.

					One key element for determining the oil's overall condition. TBN is the measurement of the reserve alkalinity of the oil's additive package. The lower the TBN in relationship to the new oil, the less its ability to clean the system and suspend contaminants. Shell's Rotella rep. recommends no less than a 3 (TBN > 5) Test Method - ASTM D-2896
Total Base Number (TBN)	mg KOH/g	7.07	5.0	3.5	Should not be less than 50% of the new oil. Rotella 15W40 = 11.5
PARTICLE COUNT					
2		Number of particles > the number shown in microns. The numbers in the 5 and 15 cells are used to cross reference to the ISO Cleanliness Rating Table to determine ISO Rating. Caterpillar Requires a 16/13 Rating which is typical for new oil. A sudden change in readings could indicate a filtration problem.			
5					
15					
20					
30					
40					
D.R. FERROGRAPHY					

The sample is flowed through a glass tube at a slight incline over a permanent magnet. Two light detectors placed in series along the front end of the tube will detect the amount of transmitted light before and after the sample has flowed through. Not hindered by particle size like the emission spectrometer. Includes non-Ferro magnetic particles of all sizes.

Small (< 5 microns)		11.2	>50	100	
Large (.1 to >300 microns)		16.0	>50	100	
INFRARED	Fourier Transform Infrared Analysis (FTIR)				
Hydroxy		0.033			
Anti-wear Loss		0.525			

Oxidation		0.497				Oxidation occurs when the base oil is attacked by oxygen. Heat, pressure, and catalytic materials like copper, accelerate the oxidation process. By-products of oxidation form lacquer deposits, corrode metal components, and increase the oil's viscosity, impairing its ability to lubricate, causing ring sticking, oil thickening, plugged filters and piston deposits. (Aeration - air is mixed with the oil causing foam, this is not Oxidation.) FTIR is an effective direct means of measuring the oil's oxidation level in a diesel engine.
Nitration		0.767				Nitration is caused by oil degradation in a reduced oxygen environment and results in nitrogenous by-products. These compounds contain acidic precursors that may combine with water to form nitrous acids in the lubricant. These acids attack the oil, reducing additive effectiveness and increasing the rate of oil degradation, which creates varnish, lacquer, sludge and engine deposits. Infrared analysis is used to directly measure nitration products in the engine lubricant. Problems here are typical to natural gas engines.

						Sulfation is the formation of compounds containing sulfur from the base oil's reaction with oxygen, heat, and sulfur (from base oil or diesel fuel). Sulfur burns to form sulfuric acid. In vapor form, passed out the exhaust, the vapor is relatively harmless. However, some vapors slip past the piston rings and valve guides into the crank case. The acid vapors condense into a liquid at 120^0C (250^0F). TBN is used to neutralize the acid and protect the internal part from corrosion. Sulfurous compounds form deposits, lacquer, varnish, and sludge. They deplete additives and can react with water to form sulfuric acids that corrode the metals and degrade the lubricant. Sulfation is also measured by FTIR. High sulfur can also cause accelerated oil consumption, with more sulfur oxides available to form acids. Causes piston sticking, corrodes valve guides, piston rings and
Oxidation/Sulfate		0.000				liners.
Oxidation – a chemical reaction between oil and oxygen causing the oil to thicken and lose its lubricating properties. Oxidation is oxygen that is absorbed into the oil. Caused mainly by high temperature operation and/or extended oil change intervals.						

Soot				1%	2%	Soot is formed during the combustion process and enters the crankcase with combustion gas blow-by. Soot is 98% carbon by weight, and has an original size of 0.01 to 0.05 microns, but tends to agglomerate to form larger particles in the crankcase. Soot levels generally increase with mileage and fuel consumption. Excess soot increases the oil's viscosity, leading to higher temperatures, higher pumping costs, power loss and the risk of lubricant starvation, especially at start-up. An oil's ability to disperse soot is critical to preventing soot-polishing wear caused by the effects of soot on the oil's anti-wear additives. If wear occurs in the valve train, fuel economy will suffer as injection timing and valve timing will move from their optimum settings. Soot indicates a dirty air cleaner, engine lug, excessive fuel delivery or repeated acceleration in the improperly set rack limiter (smoke limiter). It can also be an indicator of poor fuel, blow-by, excessive idling, rapid and excessive acceleration, poor fuel nozzle operation, cool engine temps and turbo operation.

Oil change intervals need to be based on the lubricant's ability to maintain an acceptable level of alkalinity reserve (TBN), oxidation stability, proper viscosity limits through dispersant, antioxidants and wear control.

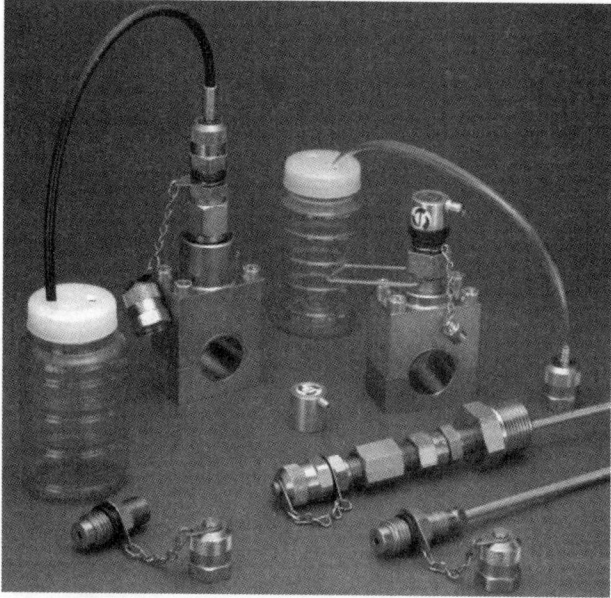

Helpful Lubrication Devices

The following are examples of some of the items you may need in improving your lubrication program. The pictures are courtesy of Checkfluid.com.

Minimess and In-line Valve

Pitot Tube with Fluid Level/Vent and Drain Functions

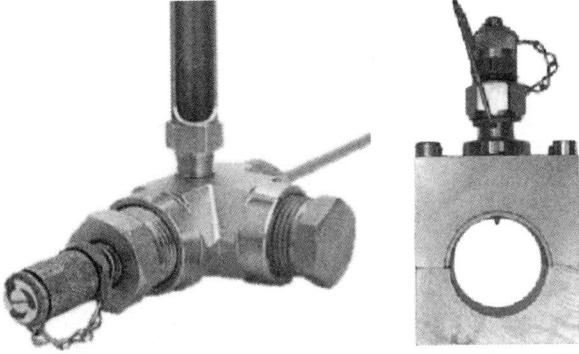

*Valve Mount – allows you to penetrate return line tubing
without having to cut and remake fittings.*

*Vacuum Pumps – used with minimess valves to draw samples
or for drawing samples directly from the reservoir.*

Grease Gun Color Coded Band Identifiers and Zerk Cap

Other Helpful Tools

Filter cart capable of transporting fluids through filters to and from reservoirs or transport containers. Can also be used to filter reservoir fluid by circulating it out, and then back into the reservoir, removing particle contaminants as well as water. The dolly cart enables movement of the oil drums.

A transfer pump/filter for smaller applications.

Desiccant Breathers to stop moisture and contaminates
from entering the system during air transference.

The following chart can assist you in determining the maximum amount of grease to apply during re-lubrication. Remember, too much grease can be as bad as not enough.

Greasing Chart

Deep Groove Ball Bearings (the last 2 digits X 5 = bore in mm)							
Bearing	Qty	Bearing	Qty	Bore Size	Re-lube - Run Hours Interval		
Series	oz		oz	inch	900 rpm	1800 rpm	3600 rpm
6204	0.10	6304	0.12	0.79	20,000	14,000	12,200
6205	0.12	6305	0.16	0.98	19,000	13,500	9,000
6206	0.15	6306	0.21	1.18	18,000	13,000	8,000
6207	0.19	6307	0.26	1.38	17,000	12,500	7,000
6208	0.23	6308	0.32	1.57	16,500	12,000	6,500
6209	0.25	6309	0.39	1.77	16,400	11,500	5,900
6210	0.28	6310	0.46	1.97	16,250	11,200	5,300
6211	0.33	6311	0.54	2.17	16,150	10,500	4,600
6212	0.38	6312	0.63	2.36	16,000	10,000	4,000
6213	0.43	6313	0.72	2.56	15,600	9,600	3,200
6214	0.47	6314	0.81	2.76	15,200	9,200	2,600
6215	0.50	6315	0.92	2.95	14,800	8,800	2,000
6216	0.55	6316	1.03	3.15	14,500	8,500	1,500
6217	0.65	6317	1.14	3.35	14,400	8,250	1,200
6218	0.74	6318	1.26	3.54	14,250	8,000	900

6219	0.84		6319	1.40	3.74		14,100	7,750	650
6220	0.95		6320	1.57	3.94		14,000	7,500	

Cylindrical Roller Bearings (N, NJ, NU)									
Bearing	Qty		Bearing	Qty	Bore Size		Re-lube - Run Hours Interval		
Series	oz			oz	inch		900 rpm	1800 rpm	3600 rpm
204	0.10		304	0.12	0.79		15,000	10,000	5,000
205	0.12		305	0.16	0.98		14,500	9,500	4,500
206	0.15		306	0.21	1.18		14,000	9,000	4,000
207	0.19		307	0.26	1.38		13,500	8,500	3,500
208	0.23		308	0.32	1.57		13,000	8,000	3,000
209	0.25		309	0.39	1.77		12,500	7,500	2,700
210	0.28		310	0.46	1.97		12,000	7,000	2,400
211	0.33		311	0.54	2.17		11,500	6,500	2,100
212	0.38		312	0.63	2.36		11,000	6,000	1,700
213	0.43		313	0.72	2.56		10,750	5,500	1,400
214	0.47		314	0.81	2.76		10,500	5,000	900
215	0.50		315	0.92	2.95		10,250	4,500	
216	0.55		316	1.03	3.15		10,000	4,000	
217	0.65		317	1.14	3.35		9,500	3,500	
218	0.74		318	1.26	3.54		9,000	3,000	
219	0.84		319	1.40	3.74		8,500	2,500	
220	0.95		320	1.57	3.94		8,000	2,000	

Re-lube Intervals based on good lithium at 167F- for every 27F rise and vertical application half interval good Polyurea would last longer. Gears more often in contamination areas.

Viscosity Comparison Chart

Remember that 40°C equals 104° F where 100°C equals 212° F. You can easily see how temperature affects viscosity.

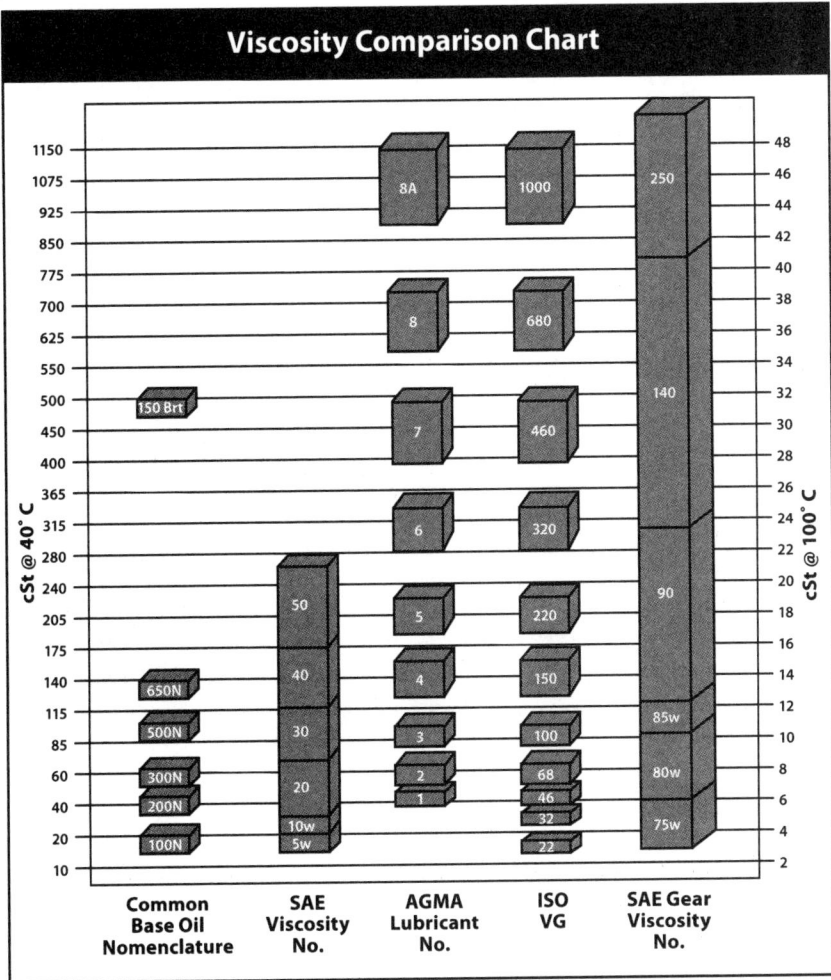

Viscosity Comparison Chart

cSt @ 40° C axis: 1150, 1075, 925, 850, 775, 700, 625, 550, 500, 450, 400, 365, 315, 280, 240, 205, 175, 140, 115, 85, 60, 40, 20, 10

cSt @ 100° C axis: 48, 46, 44, 42, 40, 38, 36, 34, 32, 30, 28, 26, 24, 22, 20, 18, 16, 14, 12, 10, 8, 6, 4, 2

Common Base Oil Nomenclature: 150 Brt, 650N, 500N, 300N, 200N, 100N

SAE Viscosity No.: 50, 40, 30, 20, 10w, 5w

AGMA Lubricant No.: 8A, 8, 7, 6, 5, 4, 3, 2, 1

ISO VG: 1000, 680, 460, 320, 220, 150, 100, 68, 46, 32, 22

SAE Gear Viscosity No.: 250, 140, 90, 85w, 80w, 75w

Relationship Between cp and SSU to cSt

This chart shows the relationship between cp and SSU to cSt.

Centipoise (cp)	Centistokes (cSt)	Saybolt Second Universal (SSU)	Typical liquid
1	1	31	Water
3.2	4	40	Milk
12.6	15.7	80	No. 4 fuel oil
16.5	20.6	100	Cream
34.6	43.2	200	Vegetable oil
88	110	500	SAE 10 oil
176	220	1000	Tomato juice
352	440	2000	SAE 30 oil
880	1100	5000	Glycerin
1561	1735	8000	SAE 50 oil
1760	2200	10,000	Honey
3000	4500	20,000	Glue
5000	6250	28,000	Mayonnaise
8640	10,800	50,000	Molasses
15,200	19,000	86,000	Sour cream
17,640	19,600	90,000	SAE 70 oil

Centipoise = centistokes x specific gravity where specific gravity is assumed to be 0.8 (except for water).

Some Simple Definitions

Abrasive	Any hard foreign material that wears down the surface of components. When abrasives enter a bearing, they can break the lubrication film and cause damage.
Absolute Filter Rating	Indicates the largest opening in the filter medium.
Adhesion	Lubrication property – the ability to adhere to lubricated surfaces.
Adhesive Wear	Galling, scoring, seizing—the two surfaces adhere to each other—indicative of loss of lubrication.
Angular Ball Bearings	A type of ball bearing in which the contact angle of the balls to the raceway allows them to accept greater thrust load than possible with non-angular ball bearings.
Anti-Friction Bearing	A type of bearing using rolling motion to support a load and reduce friction. Anti-friction bearings produce less friction than plain bearings.
Ash	The amount of inorganic material in lube oil.
Asperity (Asperities)	A microscopic peak on a surface. Even surfaces that appear smooth contain many asperities. When objects are in motion, contact between these asperities causes friction.
ASTM	American Society for Test Material—all lube tests are tested to these defined standards. Several have similar tests but produce different results—know what test is being used so accurate comparisons can be made.
Babbitt	A metal alloy often used to line plain bearings. Babbitts are commonly made of large amounts of tin with a smaller amount of antimony, copper, and lead.
Ball Bearing	A type of anti-friction bearing designed with metal balls that provide rolling motion and reduce friction between moving parts. Ball bearings are capable of operating at high speeds but cannot carry as great a load as roller-element bearings.
Bearing	A friction-reducing device that allows one moving part to glide past another moving part. Bearings operate using a sliding or rolling mechanism.
Bore	The diameter of an anti-friction bearing's shaft. The bore is also called the interior diameter (ID).
Boundary Lubrication	A type of lubrication in which the bearing and shaft rub together in partial contact and there is only a thin film of lubricant separating them.

Brinneling	A sign of damage in anti-friction bearings resulting from excessive load. Brinneling appears as indentations in the raceway.
Cage	A part found in some anti-friction bearings that separates and prevents rolling elements, such as balls, from sliding against each other.
Cylindrical Roller Bearing	The most common and basic type of roller bearing designed with cylinders of slightly greater length than width. Cylindrical bearings commonly operate in high speed, high radial load environments where thrust loads are low.
Centipoise (cps)	Absolute viscosity unit – 1 Cps = .01 poise
Centistoke (cSt)	Kinematic viscosity unit – 1 cSt = .01 stoke
Coefficient of Friction	The frictional force resisting motion of two surfaces divided by the force pressing down on the surfaces.
Consistency	Semisolids', such as grease, resistance to deformation.
Demulsibility	The ability of a fluid to separate from water when mixed.
Double-Row Bearing	A type of roller-element bearing consisting of a double-row of rolling elements. Bearings with a double row accept a greater amount of load than single-row designs. In some cases, a double-row design makes it possible for load to be carried in two directions.
Double-Row Spherical Roller Bearing	A type of spherical roller bearing that can carry 30% more radial load than single-row spherical roller bearings.
Drop Point	The temperature at which the oil completely falls out of the grease soap.
Electrical Fluting	An extreme form of electrical pitting. Fluting appears as closely spaced lines running parallel to the bearing shaft.
Electrical Pitting	A sign of damage in improperly lubricated bearings used in electrical equipment. Although it is not always visible to the naked eye, pitting appears as either frosted or darkened spots.
Extreme Pressure Additive (EP)	At high pressure, the additive prevents seizing of the surfaces. At high local temperature, the additive combines chemically with surfaces to prevent welding of the asperities.
Fluid Film Bearing	A plain bearing using hydrodynamic lubrication to operate. Fluid film bearings are also called hydrodynamic bearings.
Friction	The resistance between the contact surfaces of two objects. Friction generates heat and increases the wear between components.

Filtration (Beta)	Ratio of particles greater than a certain size entering a filter compared to the amount of particles greater than the same size leaving the filter.
Fluid Friction	The friction caused by the viscosity of a fluid.
Grooved-Race Thrust Ball Bearing	A type of thrust ball bearing designed with a grooved raceway. The grooved-race thrust bearing can operate at higher speeds and carry a higher load than flat-race thrust bearings.
Hydrodynamic Bearing	A plain bearing using hydrodynamic lubrication to operate. Hydrodynamic bearings are also called fluid film bearings.
Hydrodynamic Lubrication	A type of lubrication in which a lubricant film completely separates two surfaces in contact. Hydrodynamic lubrication is achieved when a bearing rotates quickly enough for lubrication to flow around the bearing and cover its entire surface. Hydrodynamic lubrication is also called full-fluid lubrication.
Hydrostatic Lubrication	A type of lubrication in which moving surfaces are separated externally by a highly pressurized fluid such as air, oil, or water. Hydrostatic lubrication is expensive and its use is limited.
Inner Ring	The inside portion of an anti-friction bearing that contains the rolling elements.
ISO Viscosity Grade	A number representative of the viscosity of a lubrication fluid at 40°C. ASTM D2422
Journal	The shaft of a journal bearing. The journal is softer than the outer casing of the bearing.
Journal Bearing	A type of plain bearing designed to reduce friction by supporting radial loads. Journal bearings are often used when the load is light and motion is relatively continuous, such as in crankshafts. Journal bearings are also called radial or sleeve bearings.
Kinematic Viscosity	The time required for a determined amount of fluid to flow through a capillary tube assisted only by gravity. Equals the Absolute viscosity in centipoises divided by the specific gravity.
Kingsbury Thrust Bearing	A type of plain thrust bearing capable of high thrust capacity which is able to operate even when there is some significant misalignment.
Load	The overall force that is applied to a material or structure. Bearings must support components and withstand various machine loads during operation.

Lubricant	A substance used to reduce friction between two surfaces in relative motion. Oil and grease are common industrial lubricants.
Magnetic Bearing	A bearing that uses magnetic forces to support the rotating shaft and carry a load.
Mixed-Film Lubrication	A type of lubrication in which bearings support their load partially with boundary lubrication and partially with a hydrodynamic lubrication.
Multi-Grade Oil	Oil which is capable of performing at a wider range of temperatures than single grade.
Needle Roller Bearing	A type of cylindrical bearing with long, thin rollers at least four times greater in length than their diameter. Needle roller bearings have the highest radial load capacity in relation to their height.
Oil Ring	A loose ring inside rotating equipment on the shaft used to carry oil to the bearing.
Outer Ring	The outside portion of an anti-friction bearing that contains the rolling elements.
Oxidation	Oxygen's attack on lubrication fluid – heat, light, metal catalysts, and water all accelerate the process.
Plain Bearing	A type of bearing using a sliding motion to reduce friction. Types of plain bearings include journal bearings, plain thrust bearings, and bushings.
Plain Thrust Bearing	A type of thrust bearing consisting of two parts: a wedged lower section which reduces friction and accommodates lubrication, and a rotating upper section. Plain thrust bearings are often used along with journal bearings, as in crankshafts.
Polar Compound	Chemical compound that exhibits positive charge on one end and negative on the other. Used as lubrication additives for anti-friction, anti-wear, water emulsifiers and detergents.
Pour Point	The lowest temperature oil will flow.
Raceway	The grooves within an anti-friction bearing that run along the middle of the inside and outside bearing rings. The raceway provides a path for the balls or rolling elements.
Radial Load	Force that is applied perpendicular to the axis of a bearing's shaft. Radial loads are also called rotary loads.
Reservoir	A container/tank for storing fluid for a system.

Roller	A cylindrically shaped rolling element that decreases friction when used in a rolling element anti-friction bearing.
Roller Bearing	A type of anti-friction bearing designed with rollers that provide rolling motion and reduce friction between moving parts. Roller bearings demand slower speeds than ball bearings, but they can support greater loads.
Rolling-Element Bearing	A type of bearing using rolling motion to support a load and reduce friction. Rolling-element bearings produce less friction than plain bearings. They are also called anti-friction bearings.
Rotor	A rotating component used together with a stationary part, the stator, in magnetic bearings.
Scoring	Damage done to plain bearings due to direct contact between moving parts. Scoring appears as long scratches in the direction of motion.
Silt	Particles of 5 microns or less.
Sleeve Bearing	A type of plain bearing designed to reduce friction by supporting radial loads. Sleeve bearings are often used when the load is light and motion is relatively continuous, such as in crankshafts. Sleeve bearings are also called journal bearings.
Spalling	A sign of damage in anti-friction bearings resulting from normal use or excessive load. Spalling appears as fractures in the raceway.
Specific Gravity	The weight ratio for a given liquid at a given volume compared to water for the same volume. Sg of water = 1
Spherical Roller Bearing	A type of roller bearing featuring a spherical barrel shape that allows the component to carry some thrust load in addition to high radial load.
Start-Up Friction	The initial friction caused when a machine begins operation. Start-up friction is greater than the friction that takes place once components are in motion.
Stator	A stationary component used together with a rotating part, the rotor, in magnetic bearings.
Tapered Roller Bearing	A type of roller bearing featuring tapered inner and outer ring raceways and rollers. The tapered roller bearing can withstand high radial and thrust loads.
Thin-Film Lubrication	A type of lubrication in which the lubricant film becomes too thin to separate a bearing and shaft completely. This can happen when the shaft does not rotate quickly enough to allow for hydrodynamic lubrication.

Three Body Wear	Wear caused by a particle passing between two surfaces.
Thrust Ball Bearing	A type of ball bearing designed specifically to handle thrust load.
Thrust Bearing	A type of bearing designed to reduce friction by carrying thrust or axial loads. Thrust bearings can be either plain or anti-friction bearings. The type of component supported determines the type of thrust bearing used.
Thrust Load	Force that is applied parallel to the bearing's axis. Thrust loads are also called axial or linear loads.
Viscosity	The resistance to flow of a fluid or semi-fluid substance. Viscosity is one of the most important factors to consider when selecting a lubricant.
Viscosity Index	A measure of a fluid's viscosity change with temperature. The higher the number, the less the change.
ZDDP	Zinc Dialkykldithiophosphate – an anti-wear additive found in hydraulic and lubrication fluids.

Recommended Websites:

- Skf.com – excellent bearing information including literature.
- Noria.com – training and free magazine publications.
- Hydacusa.com – filtration equipment and free cleanliness poster.
- Checkfluid.com – minimess sampling valves and more.
- Tricocorp.com – desiccant filters

References:

- Bearing handbook for Electric Motors, SKF Publication 140-430. Version 11/2005
- Bearing Installation and Maintenance Guide, SKF Publication 140-710, Version 3/2007
- Oil and your engine, Caterpillar Bulletin 2/90
- http://www.toolingu.com